The Self-Taught Computer Scientist

The beginner's guide to data structures & algorithms

Cory Althoff

WILEY

I dedicate this book to my wife, Bobbi, and my daughter, Luca. I love you both so much!

About the Author

Cory Althoff is an author, programmer, and speaker. His first book, *The Self-Taught Programmer*, has been published in seven languages and introduced the term *self-taught programmer* into the common lexicon. Book Authority named *The Self-Taught Programmer* one of the greatest programming books of all time, and *The Next Web* listed it as one of the 10 books that will help you become a better software engineer. More than 200,000 developers are part of the self-taught programmer community he created through his popular Facebook group, blog, newsletter, and Udemy course. Cory lives in California with his wife and daughter.

About the Technical Editor

Dr. Hannu Parviainen is an astrophysicist researching extrasolar planets at the Instituto de Astrofísica de Canarias, one of the world's leading astrophysics institutes and host of the largest optical telescope currently in existence. He previously worked as a postdoctoral researcher at the University of Oxford for several years. His core topics include scientific computing and modern numerical methods, and he has more than 20 years of experience in the Python programming language.

Acknowledgments

I want to give a huge thank-you to all the wonderful people who made this book possible. First up is my wife, Bobbi, the love of my life who has always supported me. I want to thank my dad, James Althoff, who has spent an enormous amount of time helping me with this book. Next up is Steve Bush: thank you so much for reading my book and giving me feedback. I also want to thank my project editor, Robyn Alvarez, and technical editor, Hannu Parviainen. Finally, I also would like to thank my editor, Devon Lewis, for making this project happen and for being incredibly flexible. Finally, I want to thank my daughter, Luca, for being the best daughter in the world and inspiring me to work as hard as I can. I love you, Luca! I couldn't have done it without all of your support. Thanks so much!

Contents at a Glance

Contents

Introduction

My journey learning to code started when I graduated from college with a political science degree. After I left school, I struggled to get a job. I didn't have the skills employers were looking for, and I watched as my friends who studied more practical subjects went on to get high-paying jobs. Meanwhile, I was stuck applying for jobs and not getting them, making no money, and feeling like a failure. So, living in Silicon Valley and being surrounded by coders, I decided to try to learn to program. Little did I know that I was about to start the craziest and most fulfilling journey of my life.

This attempt wasn't my first shot at learning to code: I had tried to learn to program in the past without success. During my freshman year of college, I took a programming class, found it impossible to understand, and quickly dropped it. Unfortunately, most schools teach Java as a first programming language, which is challenging for beginners to understand. Instead of Java, I decided to teach myself Python, one of the easiest languages for beginners to learn. Despite learning an easy-to-understand language, I still almost gave up. I had to piece together information from many different sources, which was frustrating. It also didn't help that I felt like I was on my journey alone. I didn't have a class full of students I could study with and lean on for support.

I was close to giving up when I started spending more time in online programming communities like Stack Overflow. Joining a community kept me motivated, and I began to gain momentum again. There were many ups and downs, and at times I felt like quitting, but less than a year after I made my fateful decision to learn to program, I was working as a software engineer at eBay. A year earlier, I would have been lucky to get a customer support job. Now, I was getting paid $50 an hour to program for a well-known tech company. I couldn't believe it! The best part wasn't the money, though. Once I became a software engineer, my confidence increased tenfold. After learning to code, I felt like I could accomplish anything.

After eBay, I started working at a startup in Palo Alto. Eventually, I decided to take some time off work and go on a backpacking trip to Southeast Asia. I was in the backseat of a taxi driving through the narrow streets of Seminyak, Bali, in the rain when I had an idea. Back home, people were always asking me about my experience as a software engineer. Working as a software engineer in Silicon Valley is not unusual, but I was different from many of my peers because I do not have a computer science degree.

My idea was to write a book called *The Self-Taught Programmer*: not only about programming but about everything I learned to get hired as a software engineer. In other words, I wanted to help people take the same journey I did. So I set out to create a roadmap for aspiring self-taught programmers. I spent a year writing *The Self-Taught Programmer* and self-published it. I wasn't sure if anyone would read it, and I thought most likely no one would, but I wanted to share my experience anyway. To my surprise, it sold thousands of copies in the first few months. With those sales came messages from people from around the world who were either self-taught programmers or wanted to become one.

These messages inspired me, so I decided to help solve another problem I faced learning to program: feeling alone on the journey. My solution was to create a Facebook group called Self-Taught Programmers, a place for programmers to support one another. It now has more than 60,000 members and has evolved into a supportive community filled with self-taught programmers helping each other by answering questions, trading knowledge, and sharing success stories. If you want to become part of our community, you can join at https://facebook.com/groups/selftaughtprogrammers. You can also subscribe to my newsletter at theselftaughtprogrammer.io.

When I used to post things online about working as a software engineer without a computer science degree, I would always get at least a few negative comments that it is impossible to work as a programmer without a degree. Some people would cry, "What do you self-taught programmers think you are doing? You need a degree! No company is going to take you seriously!" These days, the comments are few and far between. When they do come, I point the commenter to the Self-Taught Programmers group. We have self-taught programmers working at companies worldwide in every position, from junior software engineers to principal software engineers.

Meanwhile, my book continued to sell better than I ever thought possible and is even a popular Udemy course as well. Interacting with so many wonderful people learning to program has been an amazing and humbling experience, and I am excited to continue my journey with this book. This book is my follow-up to my first book, *The Self-Taught Programmer*, so if you haven't already read it, you should go back and read that first, unless you already understand programming basics. This book assumes you can program in Python, so if you can't, you can either go back and read my first book, take my Udemy course, or learn Python using whatever resource works best for you.

What You Will Learn

While my first book, *The Self-Taught Programmer*, introduces programming and the skills you need to learn to program professionally, this book is an introduction to computer science. Specifically, it is an introduction to data structures and algorithms. Computer science is the study of computers and how they work. When you go to college to become a software engineer, you don't major in programming; you major in computer science. Computer science students study math, computer architecture, compilers, operating systems, data structures and algorithms, network programming, and more.

Each of these topics is the subject of many very long books, and covering them all is way beyond the scope of this book. Computer science is a massive subject. You can study it your entire life and still have more to learn. This book does not aim to cover everything you would learn about if you went to school to get a computer science degree. Instead, my goal is to give you an introduction to some of the essential concepts in computer science so that you will excel in different situations as a self-taught programmer.

As a self-taught programmer, the two most important subjects for you to understand are data structures and algorithms, which is why I decided to focus this book on them. I divided this book into two parts. Part I is an introduction to algorithms. You will learn what an algorithm is and what makes one better than another, and you will learn different algorithms such as linear and binary search. Part II is an introduction to data structures. You will learn what a data structure is and study arrays, linked lists, stacks, queues, hash tables, binary trees, binary heaps, and graphs. Then, I wrap up by covering what to do once you've finished this book, including the next steps you can take and other resources to help you on your journey learning to program.

In my previous book, I explained how it doesn't make sense to study computer science before you learn to program. That doesn't mean you can ignore it, though. You have to study computer science if you want to become a successful programmer. It is as simple as this: if you don't understand computer science, you will not get hired. Almost every company that employs programmers makes them pass a technical interview as part of the application process, and technical interviews all focus on the same subject: computer science. Specifically, they focus on data structures and algorithms. To get hired at Facebook, Google, Airbnb, and all of today's hottest companies, big and small alike, you have to pass a technical interview focusing on data structures and algorithms. If you don't have a depth of knowledge in these two subjects, you will get crushed in your technical interviews. A technical interview is not something you can wing. Your potential employer will ask you detailed questions about data structures, algorithms, and more, and you better know the answers if you want to get hired.

On top of that, when you get hired for your first job, your employer and co-workers will expect you to know computer science basics. If they have to explain to you why an $O(n**3)$ algorithm is not a good solution, they won't be happy with you. That is the situation I found myself in when I got my first programming job at eBay. I was on a team with incredibly talented programmers from Stanford, Berkley, and Cal Tech. They all had a deep understanding of computer science, and I felt insecure and out of place. As a self-taught programmer, studying computer science will help you avoid this fate.

Furthermore, studying data structures and algorithms will make you a better programmer. Feedback loops are the key to mastering a skill. A feedback loop is when you practice a skill and get immediate feedback on whether you did a good job. When you are practicing programming, there is no feedback loop. For example, if you create a website, the website may work, but your code could be horrible. There is no feedback loop to tell you if your code is any good or not. When you are studying algorithms, however, that is not the case. There are many famous computer science algorithms, which means you can write code to solve a problem, compare your result to the existing algorithm, and instantly know whether you wrote a decent solution. Practicing with a positive feedback loop like this will improve your coding skills.

The biggest mistake I made as a new self-taught programmer attempting to break into the software industry was not spending enough time studying data structures and algorithms. If I had spent more time studying them, my journey would have been much more manageable. You don't have to make that mistake!

As I mentioned, computer science is a massive subject. There is a reason why computer science students spend four years studying it: there is a lot to learn. You may not have four years to spend studying computer science. Fortunately, you don't have to. This book covers many of the most important things you need to know to have a successful career as a software engineer. Reading this book will not replace a four-year computer science degree. However, if you read this book and practice the examples, you will have a solid foundation for passing a technical interview. You will start feeling comfortable on a team of computer science majors, and you will also significantly improve as a programmer.

Who Is This Book For?

So I've convinced you that self-taught programmers can program professionally and that you need to study computer science, especially data structures and algorithms. But does that mean you can't read this book unless you are learning to program outside of school? Of course not! Everyone is welcome in the self-taught community! My first book was surprisingly popular with college students. A few college professors even contacted me and told me they were teaching their programming classes using my book.

College students studying computer science often ask me if they should drop out. My goal is to inspire as many people to learn to program as possible. That means letting people know it is possible to program professionally without a degree in computer science. If you are already in school studying computer science, that works too, and no, you should not drop out. Stay in school, kids! Even if you are in school, you can still be part of the self-taught community by applying our "always be learning" mindset to your schoolwork and going above and beyond to learn even more than your professors teach you.

So how do you know if you are ready to study computer science? Easy. If you already know how to program, you are ready! I wrote this book for anyone who wants to learn more about computer science. Whether you are reading this book to fill in the gaps in your knowledge, prepare for a technical interview, feel knowledgeable at your job, or become a better programmer, I wrote this book for you.

Self-Taught Success Stories

I got hired as a software engineer without a degree, and I hear new success stories from self-taught programmers every day. As a self-taught programmer, you absolutely can have a successful career as a software engineer without a degree. I know this can be a sticking point for some people, so before we dive into computer science, I want to share a few self-taught programmer success stories from my Facebook group.

Matt Munson

First up is Matt Munson, a member of the Self-Taught Programmers Facebook group. Here is his story in his own words:

It all started when I lost my job at Fintech. To make ends meet, I started working odd jobs: cutting lenses for glasses, fixing and tuning cars, working as a carnie, and doing small side programming projects. Despite my best efforts, after a few months, I lost my apartment. This is the story of how I escaped homelessness by becoming a programmer.

When I lost my job, I was enrolled in school. After I lost my house, I kept doing schoolwork out of my car and tent for a couple of months. My family wasn't able to help me. They didn't understand minimum wage jobs don't pay anywhere near enough to feed one person and keep gas in the tank while keeping a roof over your head. Nonetheless, I was still unwilling to reach out to my friends for help. In September, I sold my truck, cashed what I had left in a 401(k), and drove the 1,800 or so miles from my hometown in Helena, Montana, to take my chances in Austin, Texas.

Within a week, I had two or three interviews, but no companies wanted to take a chance on a homeless guy, skilled or not. After a few months of this, I had friends and strangers donating to my GoFundMe to try to help me get back on my feet. At this point, I was eating about once a day, seldom anything good, in any sense of the word. My only shot at getting out of this situation was becoming a programmer.

Finally, I decided to do one last push. I sent out my résumé en masse to any job I remotely had a chance of being qualified for. The next day, a small startup called me for an interview. I did my best to look decent. I shaved, put on clean clothes, tied my hair back, showered (a hell of a task for the homeless), and showed up. I came clean, explained my situation, explained why I took my chances here in Austin, did my best during the interview to show I may not be the best as I stood there at that moment, but given an opportunity, I would work my ass off to show that one day I could be the best.

I left feeling like I bombed the interview. I thought maybe my honesty had sunk my chances, but a week and a half later, after feeling like giving up entirely, the startup called me back in for a second interview.

When I showed up, it was only the big dog. The boss said he was impressed by my honesty, and he wanted to give me a chance. He told me I had a decent foundation, and I was like a box: a sturdy but relatively empty box. He thought I was sturdy enough to handle anything they threw at me, and I would learn on the job. Finally, he told me I would start on December 6.

One year later, I live in a much nicer apartment than before becoming a programmer. I am respected among my co-workers, and they even ask my opinion on significant company matters. You can do or be anything. Never be afraid to try, even if it means taking a real chance at everything falling apart.

Tianni Myers

Next up is Tianni Myers, who read *The Self-Taught Programmer* and emailed me the following story about his journey learning to code outside of school:

My self-taught journey started in a web design class I took in college while working toward a bachelor's degree in media communications. At the time, I was interested in writing and had dreams of working in marketing. My goals shifted after deciding to learn to program. I'm writing to share my self-taught story about how I went from retail cashier to a junior web developer in 12 months.

I started out learning the basics of HTML and CSS on Code Academy. I wrote my first Python program, a numbers game; the computer picked a random number, and the user had three tries to guess the correct one. That project and Python got me excited about computers.

My mornings started at 4 a.m., making a cup of coffee. I spent 6 to 10 hours a day reading programming books and writing code. At the time, I was 21, and I worked part-time at Goodwill to make ends meet. I had never been happier because I spent most of my day doing what I loved, which was building and creating various programming languages as my tools.

I was on Indeed one day casually applying for jobs. I wasn't expecting to get a response, but I did a few days later from a marketing agency. I did a SQL assessment on Indeed followed by a phone interview, then a code assessment, and soon after an in-person interview. During my interview, the web development director and two senior developers sat down and reviewed my answers for the code assessment. I felt good because they were blown away by some of my answers and pleasantly surprised when I told them I was self-taught. They told me some of my answers were better than ones given by senior developers that they had previously given the same code assessment. Two weeks later, they hired me.

If you can put in the work and get through the pain, then you can make your dreams come true as I did.

Getting Started

The code examples in this book are in Python. I chose Python because it is one of the easiest programming languages to read. Throughout the book, I formatted the code examples like this:

```
for i in range(100):
    print("Hello, World!")

>> Hello, World!
>> Hello, World!
>> Hello, World!
```

The text `# http://tinyurl.com/h4qntgk` contains a URL that takes you to a web page that contains the code from it, so you can easily copy and paste it into Python's IDLE text editor if you are having problems getting the code to run. The text that comes after `>>` is the output of Python's interactive shell. Ellipses after an output (...) mean "and so on." If there is no `>>` after an example, it means either the program doesn't produce any output or I am explaining a concept, and the output is not important. Anything in a paragraph in `monospaced font` is some form of code or code output or programming jargon.

Installing Python

To follow the examples in this book, you need to have Python version 3 installed. You can download Python for Windows and Unix at `http://python.org/downloads`. If you are on Ubuntu, Python 3 comes installed by default. Make sure you download Python 3, not Python 2. Some of the examples in this book will not work if you are using Python 2.

Python is available for 32-bit and 64-bit computers. If you purchased your computer after 2007, it is most likely a 64-bit computer. If you aren't sure, an Internet search should help you figure it out.

If you are on Windows or a Mac, download the 32- or 64-bit version of Python, open the file, and follow the instructions. You can also visit `http://theselftaughtprogrammer.io/installpython` for videos explaining how to install Python on each operating system.

Troubleshooting

If you are having difficulties installing Python, please post a message in the Self-Taught Programmers Facebook group. You can find it at `https://facebook.com/groups/selftaughtprogrammers`. When you post code in the Self-Taught Programmer Facebook group (or anywhere else online asking for help), make sure to put your code in a GitHub Gist. Never send a screenshot of your code. When people help you, they often need to run your program themselves. When you send a screenshot, they have to type all of your code by hand, whereas if you send your code in a GitHub Gist, they can quickly copy and paste it into their IDE.

Challenges

Many of the chapters in this book end with a coding challenge for you to solve. These challenges are meant to test your understanding of the material, make you a better programmer, and help prepare you for a technical interview. You can find the solutions to all of the challenges in this book on GitHub at `https://github.com/calthoff/tstcs_challenge_solutions`.

As you are reading this book and solving the challenges, I encourage you to share your wins with the self-taught community by using `#selftaughtcoder` on Twitter. Whenever you feel like you are making exciting progress on your journey learning to code, send a motivational tweet using `#selftaughtcoder` so other people in the community can get motivated by your progress. Feel free to also tag me: `@coryalthoff`.

Sticking with It

There is one last thing I want to cover before you dive into learning computer science. If you are reading this book, you've already taught yourself to program. As you know, the most challenging part about picking up a new skill like programming isn't the difficulty of the material: it is sticking with it. Sticking with learning new things is something I struggled with for years until I finally learned a trick that I would like to share with you, called Don't Break the Chain.

Jerry Seinfeld invented Don't Break the Chain. He came up with it when he was crafting his first stand-up comedy routine. First, he hung a calendar up in his room. Then, if he wrote a joke at the end of each day, he gave himself a red X (I like the idea of green check marks better) on the calendar for that day. That's it. That is the entire trick, and it is incredibly powerful.

Once you start a chain (two or more green check marks in a row), you will not want to break it. Two green check marks in a row become five green check marks in a row. Then 10. Then 20. The longer your streak gets, the harder it will be for you to break it. Imagine it is the end of the month, and you are looking at your calendar. You have 29 green check marks. You need only one more for a perfect month. There is no way you won't accomplish your task that day. Or as Jerry Seinfeld describes it:

> After a few days, you'll have a chain. Just keep at it, and the chain will grow longer every day. You'll like seeing that chain, especially when you get a few weeks under your belt. Your only job next is to not break the chain.

My dedication to preserving one of my chains has led me to do crazy things, like going to the gym in the middle of the night, to keep it intact. There is no better feeling than looking back at the calendar page containing your first perfect month and seeing it filled with green check marks. If you are ever in a rut, you can always look back at that page and think about the month where you did everything right.

Technical books are hard to get through. I've lost count of how many I've abandoned partway through. I tried to make this book as fun and easy to read as possible, but to give yourself extra insurance, try using Don't Break the Chain to ensure you finish this book. I also partnered with monday.com to create a free Self-Taught Programmer template and app that keeps track of your coding streaks for you. You can try it at https://hey.monday.com/CoryAlthoff.

With that said, are you ready to study computer science?
Let's get started!

Introduction to Algorithms

What Is an Algorithm?

> *Whether you want to uncover the secrets of the universe or you just want to pursue a career*
> *in the 21st century, basic computer programming is an essential skill to learn.*
>
> Stephen Hawking

An **algorithm** is a sequence of steps that solves a problem. For example, one algorithm for making scrambled eggs is to crack three eggs over a bowl, whisk them, pour them into a pan, heat the pan on a stove, stir them, and remove them from the pan once they are no longer runny. This section of the book is all about algorithms. You will learn algorithms you can use to solve problems such as finding prime numbers. You will also learn how to write a new, elegant type of algorithm and how to search and sort data.

In this chapter, you will learn how to compare two algorithms to help you analyze them. It is important for a programmer to understand why one algorithm may be better than another because programmers spend most of their time writing algorithms and deciding what data structures to use with them. If you have no idea why you should choose one algorithm over another, you will not be a very effective programmer, so this chapter is critical.

While algorithms are a fundamental concept in computer science, computer scientists have not agreed on a formal definition. There are many competing definitions, but Donald Knuth's is among the best known. He describes an algorithm as a definite, effective, and finite process that receives input and produces output based on this input.

Definiteness means that the steps are clear, concise, and unambiguous.

Effectiveness means that you can perform each operation precisely to solve the problem.

Finiteness means that the algorithm stops after a finite number of steps.

A common addition to this list is *correctness*. An algorithm should always produce the same output for a given input, and this output should be the correct answer to the problem the algorithm solves.

Most, but not all, algorithms fulfill these requirements, and some of the exceptions are important. For example, when you create a random number generator, your goal is to generate randomness so someone can't use the input to guess the output. Also, many algorithms in data science are not strict about correctness. For example, it may be sufficient for an algorithm to estimate output, as long as the estimate's uncertainty is known. In most cases, however, your algorithms should fulfill all the previous requirements. If you write an algorithm for making scrambled eggs, the user might not be happy if, occasionally, the algorithm produces an omelet or boiled eggs instead.

Analyzing Algorithms

There is often more than one algorithm we can use to solve a problem. For example, there are several different ways to sort a list. When several algorithms solve a problem, how do you know which one is best? Is it the simplest? The fastest? The smallest? Or something else?

One way to judge an algorithm is by its run time. An algorithm's **run time** is the amount of time it takes your computer to execute an algorithm written in a programming language like Python. For example, here is an algorithm in Python that counts from 1 to 5 and prints each number:

```
for i in range(1, 6):
    print(i)
```

You can measure this algorithm's run time using Python's built-in time module to track how long your computer takes to execute it:

```
import time

start = time.time()
for i in range(1, 6):
    print(i)
end = time.time()
print(end - start)

>> 1
>> 2
>> 3
>> 4
>> 5
>> 0.15141820907592773
```

When you run your program, it prints the numbers from 1 to 5 and outputs the time it took to execute. In this case, it took 0.15 seconds.

Now, rerun your program:

```
import time

start = time.time()
for i in range(1, 6):
```

```
    print(i)
end = time.time()
print(end - start)

>> 1
>> 2
>> 3
>> 4
>> 5
>> 0.14856505393981934
```

The second time you run your program, you should see a different run time. If you rerun your program, you will see yet another run time. The algorithm's run time keeps changing because the available processing power your computer has when it runs your program varies and in turn affects the program's run time.

Further, this algorithm's run time would be different on another computer. If you run it on a computer with less processing power, it would be slower, whereas it would be faster on a more powerful computer. Furthermore, this program's run time is affected by the programming language you wrote it in. For example, the run time would be faster if you run this same program in C because C can be faster than Python.

Because an algorithm's run time is affected by so many different variables, such as your computer's processing power and the programming language, run time is not an effective way to compare two algorithms. Instead, computer scientists compare algorithms by looking at the number of steps they require. You can input the number of steps involved in an algorithm into a formula that can compare two or more algorithms without considering the programming language or computer. Let's take a look at an example. Here is your program from earlier that counts from 1 to 5:

```
for i in range(1, 6):
    print(i)
```

Your program takes five steps to complete (it goes through a loop five times and prints i each time). You can express the number of steps your algorithm requires with this equation:

```
f(n) = 5
```

If you make your program more complicated, your equation will change. For example, you may want to keep track of the sum of all the numbers you are printing:

```
count = 0
for i in range(1, 6):
    print(i)
    count += i
```

Now, your algorithm takes 11 steps to complete. First, it assigns the variable count to zero. Then, it prints five numbers and increments five times $(1 + 5 + 5 = 11)$.

This is the new equation for your algorithm:

```
f(n) = 11
```

What happens if you change the 6 in your code to a variable?

```
count = 0
for i in range(1, n):
    print(i)
    count += i
```

Your equation changes to this:

```
f(n) = 1 + 2n
```

Now the number of steps your algorithm takes depends on whatever the value of n is. The 1 in the equation represents the first step: count = 0. Then, there are two times n steps after that. For example, if n is 5, f(n) = 1 + 2 × 5. Computer scientists call the variable n in an equation that describes the number of steps in an algorithm the **size of the problem**. In this case, you could say the time it takes to solve a problem of size n is $1 + 2n$, or in mathematical notation, $T(n) = 1 + 2n$.

An equation describing the number of steps in an algorithm is not very helpful, however, because, among other things, you can't always reliably count the number of steps in an algorithm. For example, if an algorithm has many conditional statements, you have no way of knowing which of them will execute in advance. The good news is, as a computer scientist, you don't care about the exact number of steps in an algorithm. What you want to know is how an algorithm performs as n gets bigger. Most algorithms perform fine on a small data set but may be a disaster with larger data sets. Even the most inefficient algorithm will perform well if n is 1. In the real world, however, n will probably not be 1. It may be several hundred thousand, a million, or more.

The important thing to know about an algorithm is not the exact number of steps it will take but rather an approximation of the number of steps it will take as n gets bigger. As n gets larger, one part of the equation will overshadow the rest of the equation to the point that everything else becomes irrelevant. Take a look at this Python code:

```
def print_it(n):
    # loop 1
    for i in range(n):
        print(i)
    # loop 2
    for i in range(n):
```

```
        print(i)
        for j in range(n):
            print(j)
            for h in range(n):
                print(h)
```

What part of this program is most important for determining how many steps your algorithm takes to complete? You may think both parts of the function (the first loop and the second loop containing other loops) are important. After all, if *n* is 10,000, your computer will print many numbers in both loops.

It turns out that the following code is irrelevant when you are talking about your algorithm's efficiency:

```
# loop 1
for i in range(n):
    print(i)
```

To understand why, you need to look at what happens as *n* gets bigger.

Here is the equation for the number of steps in your algorithm:

```
T(n) = n + n**3
```

When you have two nested `for` loops that take *n* steps, it translates to *n***2 (*n* to the second power) because if *n* is 10, you have to do 10 steps twice, or 10**2. Three nested `for` loops are always *n***3 for the same reason. In this equation, when *n* is 10, the first loop in your program takes 10 steps, and the second loop takes 10^3 steps, which is 1,000. When *n* is 1,000, the first loop takes 1,000 steps, and the second loop takes $1,000^3$, which is 1 billion.

See what happened? As *n* gets bigger, the second part of your algorithm grows so much more quickly that the first part becomes irrelevant. For example, if you needed this program to work for 100,000,000 database records, you wouldn't care about how many steps the first part of the equation takes because the second part will take exponentially more steps. With 100,000,000 records, the second part of the algorithm would take more than a septillion steps, which is 1 followed by 24 zeros, so it is not a reasonable algorithm to use. The first 100,000,000 steps aren't relevant to your decision.

Because the important part of an algorithm is the part that grows the fastest as *n* gets bigger, computer scientists use big O notation to express an algorithm's efficiency instead of a T(*n*) equation. **Big O notation** is a mathematical notation that describes how an algorithm's time or space requirements (you will learn about space requirements later) increase as the size of *n* increases.

Computer scientists use big O notation to create an order-of-magnitude function from T(*n*). An **order of magnitude** is a class in a classification system where each class is many times greater or smaller than the one before. In an order-of-magnitude function, you use the part of T(*n*) that dominates the equation and ignore everything else. The part of T(*n*) that dominates the equation is an algorithm's order of magnitude. These are the most commonly used classifications for order of magnitude in big O notation, sorted from the best (most efficient) to worst (least efficient):

Constant time

Logarithmic time

Linear time

Log-linear time

Quadratic time

Cubic time

Exponential time

Each order of magnitude describes an algorithm's time complexity. **Time complexity** is the maximum number of steps an algorithm takes to complete as n gets larger.

Let's take a look at each order of magnitude.

Constant Time

The most efficient order of magnitude is called *constant time complexity*. An algorithm runs in **constant time** when it requires the same number of steps regardless of the problem's size. The big O notation for constant complexity is O(1).

Say you run an online bookstore and give a free book to your first customer each day. You store your customers in a list called customers. Your algorithm might look like this:

```
free_books = customers[0]
```

Your T(n) equation looks like this:

```
T(n) = 1
```

Your algorithm requires one step no matter how many customers you have. If you have 1,000 customers, your algorithm takes one step. If you have 10,000 customers, your algorithm takes one step, and if you have a trillion customers, your algorithm takes only one step.

When you graph constant time complexity with the number of inputs on the x-axis and the number of steps on the y-axis, the graph is flat (Figure 1.1).

As you can see, the number of steps your algorithm takes to complete does not get larger as the problem's size increases. Therefore, it is the most efficient algorithm you can write because your algorithm's run time does not change as your data sets grow larger.

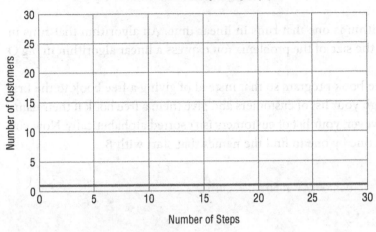

Figure 1.1: Constant complexity

Logarithmic Time

Logarithmic time is the second most efficient time complexity. An algorithm takes **logarithmic time** when its run time grows in proportion to the logarithm of the input size. You see this time complexity in algorithms such as a binary search that can discard many values at each iteration. If this is not clear, don't worry, because we will discuss this in depth later in the book. You express a logarithmic algorithm in big O notation as $O(\log n)$.

Figure 1.2 shows what it looks like when you plot a logarithmic algorithm.

The required number of steps grows more slowly in a logarithmic algorithm as the data set gets larger.

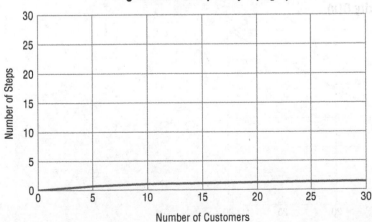

Figure 1.2: Logarithmic complexity

Linear Time

The next most efficient type of algorithm is one that runs in linear time. An algorithm that runs in **linear time** grows at the same rate as the size of the problem. You express a linear algorithm in big O notation as $O(n)$.

Suppose you must modify your free book program so that instead of giving a free book to the first customer of the day, you iterate through your list of customers and give them a free book if their name starts with the letter B. This time, however, your list of customers isn't sorted alphabetically. Now you are forced to iterate through your list one by one to find the names that start with B.

```
free_book = False
customers = ["Lexi", "Britney", "Danny", "Bobbi", "Chris"]
for customer in customers:
    if customer[0] == 'B':
        print(customer)
```

When your customer list contains five items, your program takes five steps to complete. For a list of 10 customers, your program requires 10 steps; for 20 customers, 29 steps; and so on.

This is the equation for the time complexity of this program:

```
f(n) = 1 + 1 + n
```

And in big O notation, you can ignore the constants and focus on the part that dominates the equation:

```
O(n) = n
```

In a linear algorithm, as n gets bigger, the number of steps your algorithm takes increases by however much n increases (Figure 1.3).

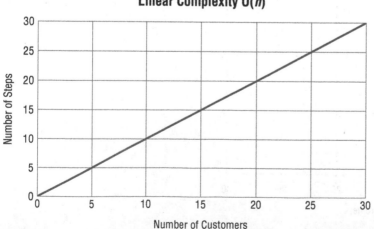

Linear Complexity O(n)

Figure 1.3: Linear complexity

Log-Linear Time

An algorithm that runs in **log-linear time** grows as a combination (multiplication) of logarithmic and linear time complexities. For example, a log-linear algorithm might evaluate an O(log n) operation n times. In big O notation, you express a log-linear algorithm as O(n log n). Log-linear algorithms often divide a data set into smaller parts and process each piece independently. For example, many of the more efficient sorting algorithms you will learn about later, such as merge sort, are log-linear.

Figure 1.4 shows what a log-linear algorithm looks like when you plot it on a graph.

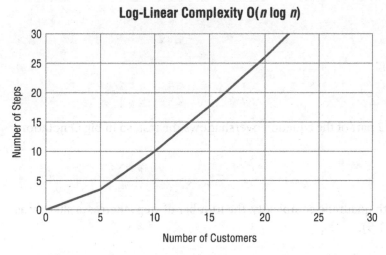

Figure 1.4: Log-linear complexity

As you can see, log-linear complexity is not as efficient as linear time. However, its complexity does not grow nearly as quickly as quadratic, which you will learn about next.

Quadratic Time

After log-linear, the next most efficient time complexity is quadratic time. An algorithm runs in **quadratic time** when its performance is directly proportional to the problem's size squared. In big O notation, you express a quadratic algorithm as O($n**2$).

Here is an example of an algorithm with quadratic complexity:

```
numbers = [1, 2, 3, 4, 5]
for i in numbers:
    for j in numbers:
        x = i * j
        print(x)
```

This algorithm multiplies every number in a list of numbers by every other number, stores the result in a variable, and prints it.

In this case, *n* is the size of your numbers list. The equation for this algorithm's time complexity is as follows:

```
f(n) = 1 + n * n * (1 + 1)
```

The (1 + 1) in the equation comes from the multiplication and print statement. You repeat the multiplication and print statement *n* * *n* times with your two nested for loops. You can simplify the equation to this:

```
f(n) = 1 + (1 + 1) * n**2
```

which is the same as the following:

```
f(n) = 1 + 2 * n**2
```

As you may have guessed, the *n***2 part of the equation overshadows the rest, so in big O notation, the equation is as follows:

```
O(n) = n**2
```

When you graph an algorithm with quadratic complexity, the number of steps increases sharply as the problem's size increases (Figure 1.5).

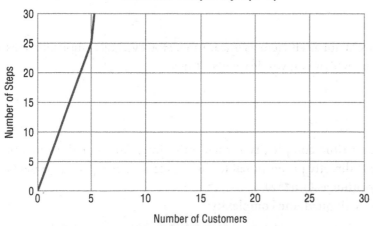

Figure 1.5: Quadratic complexity

As a general rule, if your algorithm contains two nested loops running from 1 to n (or from 0 to $n - 1$), its time complexity will be at least $O(n**2)$. Many sorting algorithms such as insertion and bubble sort (which you will learn about later in the book) follow quadratic time.

Cubic Time

After quadratic comes cubic time complexity. An algorithm runs in **cubic time** when its performance is directly proportional to the problem's size cubed. In big O notation, you express a cubic algorithm as $O(n**3)$. An algorithm with a cubic complexity is similar to quadratic, except n is raised to the third power instead of the second.

Here is an algorithm with cubic time complexity:

```
numbers = [1, 2, 3, 4, 5]
for i in numbers:
    for j in numbers:
        for h in numbers:
            x = i + j + h
            print(x)
```

The equation for this algorithm is as follows:

```
f(n) = 1 + n * n * n * (1 + 1)
```

Or as follows:

```
f(n) = 1 + 2 * n**3
```

Like an algorithm with quadratic complexity, the most critical part of this equation is $n**3$, which grows so quickly it makes the rest of the equation, even if it included $n**2$, irrelevant. So, in big O notation, quadratic complexity is as follows:

```
O(n) = n**3
```

While two nested loops are a sign of quadratic time complexity, having three nested loops running from 0 to n means that the algorithm will follow cubic time. You will most likely encounter cubic time complexity if your work involves data science or statistics.

Both quadratic and cubic time complexities are special cases of a larger family of polynomial time complexities. An algorithm that runs in **polynomial time** scales as $O(n^{**}a)$, where $a = 2$ for quadratic time and $a = 3$ for cubic time. When designing your algorithms, you generally want to avoid polynomial scaling when possible because the algorithms can get very slow as n gets larger. Sometimes you can't escape polynomial scaling, but you can find comfort knowing that the polynomial complexity is still not the worst case, by far.

Exponential Time

The honor of the worst time complexity goes to exponential time complexity. An algorithm that runs in **exponential time** contains a constant raised to the size of the problem. In other words, an algorithm with exponential time complexity takes c raised to the nth power steps to complete. The big O notation for exponential complexity is $O(c^{**}n)$, where c is a constant. The value of the constant doesn't matter. What matters is that n is in the exponent.

Fortunately, you won't encounter exponential complexity often. One example of exponential complexity involving trying to guess a numerical password consisting of n decimal digits by testing every possible combination is $O(10^{**}n)$.

Here is an example of password guessing with $O(10^{**}n)$ complexity:

```
pin = 931
n = len(pin)
for i in range(10**n):
    if i == pin:
        print(i)
```

The number of steps this algorithm takes to complete grows incredibly fast as n gets larger. When n is 1, this algorithm takes 10 steps. When n is 2, it takes 100 steps. When n is 3, it takes 1,000 steps. As you can see, at first, an exponential algorithm looks like it doesn't grow very quickly. However, eventually, its growth explodes. Guessing a password with 8 decimal digits takes 100 million steps, and guessing a password with 10 decimal digits takes more than 10 billion steps. Exponential scaling is the reason why it is so important to create long passwords. If someone tries to guess your password using a program like this, they can easily guess it if your password is four digits. However, if your password is 20 digits, it is impossible to crack because the program will take longer to run than a person's life span.

This solution to guessing a password is an example of a brute-force algorithm. A **brute-force algorithm** is a type of algorithm that tests every possible option. Brute-force algorithms are not usually efficient and should be your last resort.

Figure 1.6 compares the efficiency of the algorithms we have discussed.

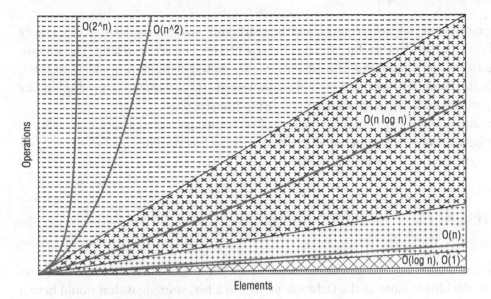

Figure 1.6: Big O complexity chart

Best-Case vs. Worst-Case Complexity

An algorithm's performance can change depending on different factors, such as the type of data you are working with. Because of this, when you evaluate an algorithm's performance, you need to consider its best-, worst-, and average-case complexities. An algorithm's **best-case complexity** is how it performs with ideal input, and an algorithm's **worst-case complexity** is how it performs in the worst possible scenario for it. An algorithm's **average-case complexity** is how it performs on average.

For example, if you have to search one by one through a list, you may get lucky and find what you are looking for after checking the first item in your list. That would be the best-case complexity. However, if the item you are looking for isn't in the list, you would have to search the entire list, which is the worst-case complexity.

If you have to search through a list one by one a hundred times, on average you will find what you are looking for in O(n/2) time, which is the same as O(n) time in big-O notation. When comparing algorithms, you often start by looking at the average-case complexity. If you want to do a deeper analysis, you can also compare their best-case and worst-case complexities.

Space Complexity

Computers have finite resources such as memory, so in addition to thinking about an algorithm's time complexity, you should consider its resource usage. **Space complexity** is the amount of memory space your algorithm needs and includes fixed space, data structure space, and temporary space. **Fixed space** is the amount of memory your program requires, and **data structure space** is the amount of memory your program needs to store the data set, for example, the size of a list you are searching. The amount of memory your algorithm uses to hold this data depends on the amount of input the problem requires. **Temporary space** is the amount of memory your algorithm needs for intermediary processing, for example, if your algorithm needs to temporarily copy a list to transfer data.

You can apply the time complexity concepts you learned earlier to space complexity. For example, you can calculate a factorial of n (a product of all positive integers less than or equal to n) using an algorithm that has a constant, $O(1)$, space complexity:

```
x = 1
n = 5
for i in range(1, n + 1):
    x = x * i
```

The space complexity is constant because the amount of space your algorithm needs does not grow as n gets larger. If you decided to store all the factorials up to n in a list, your algorithm would have a linear space complexity, $O(n)$:

```
x = 1
n = 5
a_list = []
for i in range(1, n + 1):
    a_list.append(x)
    x = x * i
```

Your algorithm's space complexity is $O(n)$ because the amount of space it uses grows at the same pace as n.

Like with time complexity, the acceptable level of space complexity for an algorithm depends on the situation. In general, though, the less space an algorithm requires, the better.

Why Is This Important?

As a computer scientist, you need to understand the different orders of magnitude to optimize your algorithms. When you are trying to improve an algorithm, you should focus on changing its order of magnitude instead of improving it in other ways. For example, say you have an $O(n**2)$ algorithm that uses two for loops. Instead of optimizing what happens inside your loops, it is much more important to determine whether you can rewrite your algorithm so that it doesn't have two nested for loops and thus has a smaller order of magnitude.

If you can solve the problem by writing an algorithm with two unnested for loops, your algorithm will be $O(n)$, which will make a massive difference in its performance. That change will make a much bigger difference in your algorithm's performance than any efficiency gains you could get by tweaking your $O(n**2)$ algorithm. However, it is also important to think about best- and worst-case scenarios for your algorithm. Maybe you have an $O(n**2)$ algorithm, but in its best-case scenario, it is $O(n)$, and your data happens to fit its best-case scenario. In that case, the algorithm may be a good choice.

The decisions you make about algorithms can have enormous consequences in the real world. For example, say you are a web developer responsible for writing an algorithm that responds to a customer's web request. Whether you decide to write a constant or quadratic algorithm could make the difference between your website loading in less than one second, making your customer happy, and taking more than a minute, which may cause you to lose customers before the request loads.

Vocabulary

algorithm: A sequence of steps that solves a problem.

run time: The amount of time it takes your computer to execute an algorithm written in a programming language like Python.

size of the problem: The variable n in an equation that describes the number of steps in an algorithm.

big O notation: A mathematical notation that describes how an algorithm's time or space requirements increase as the size of n increases.

order of magnitude: A class in a classification system where each class is many times greater or smaller than the one before.

time complexity: The maximum number of steps an algorithm takes to complete as n gets larger.

constant time: An algorithm runs in constant time when it requires the same number of steps regardless of the problem's size.

logarithmic time: An algorithm runs in logarithmic time when its run time grows in proportion to the logarithm of the input size.

linear time: An algorithm runs in linear time when it grows at the same rate as the problem's size.

log-linear time: An algorithm runs in log-linear time when it grows as a combination (multiplication) of logarithmic and linear time complexities.

quadratic time: An algorithm runs in quadratic time when its performance is directly proportional to the square of the size of the problem.

cubic time: An algorithm runs in cubic time when its performance is directly proportional to the cube of the size of the problem.

polynomial time: An algorithm runs in polynomial time when it scales as $O(n**a)$, where $a = 2$ for quadratic time and $a = 3$ for cubic time.

exponential time: An algorithm runs in exponential time when it contains a constant raised to the problem's size.

brute-force algorithm: A type of algorithm that tests every possible option.

best-case complexity: How an algorithm performs with ideal input.

worst-case complexity: How an algorithm performs in the worst possible scenario for it.

average-case complexity: How an algorithm performs on average.

space complexity: The amount of memory space an algorithm needs.

fixed space: The amount of memory a program requires.

data structure space: The amount of memory a program requires to store the data set.

temporary space: The amount of memory an algorithm needs for intermediary processing, for example, if your algorithm needs to temporarily copy a list to transfer data.

Challenge

1. Find a program you've written in the past. Go through it and write down the time complexities for the different algorithms in it.

2

Recursion

To understand recursion, one must first understand recursion.

Anonymous

An **iterative algorithm** solves problems by repeating steps over and over, typically using a loop. Most of the algorithms you've written in your programming journey so far are likely iterative algorithms. **Recursion** is a method of problem-solving where you solve smaller instances of the problem until you arrive at a solution. Recursive algorithms rely on functions that call themselves. Any problem you can solve with an iterative algorithm, you can also solve with a recursive one; however, sometimes, a recursive algorithm is a more elegant solution.

You write a recursive algorithm inside of a function or method that calls itself. The code inside the function changes the input and passes in a new, different input the next time the function calls itself. Because of this, the function must have a **base case**: a condition that ends a recursive algorithm to stop it from continuing forever. Each time the function calls itself, it moves closer to the base case. Eventually, the base case condition is satisfied, the problem is solved, and the function stops calling itself. An algorithm that follows these rules satisfies the three laws of recursion:

- A recursive algorithm must have a base case.
- A recursive algorithm must change its state and move toward the base case.
- A recursive algorithm must call itself recursively.

To help you understand how a recursive algorithm works, let's take a look at finding the factorial of a number using both a recursive and iterative algorithm. The **factorial** of a number is the product of all positive integers less than or equal to the number. For example, the factorial of 5 is $5 \times 4 \times 3 \times 2 \times 1$.

```
5! = 5 * 4 * 3 * 2 * 1
```

Here is an iterative algorithm that calculates the factorial of a number, n:

```
def factorial(n):
```

```
the_product = 1
while n > 0:
    the_product *= n
    n = n - 1
return the_product
```

Your function, `factorial`, accepts the number, n, that you are using in your calculation.

```
def factorial(n):
```

Inside your function, you define a variable, `the_product`, and set it to 1. You use `the_product` to keep track of the product as you multiply n by the numbers preceding it, for example, 5 * 4 * 3 * 2 * 1. Next, you use a `while` loop to iterate backward from n to 1 while keeping track of the product.

```
while n > 0:
    the_product *= n
    n = n - 1
```

At the end of your `while` loop, you return `the_product`, which contains the factorial of n.

```
return the_product
```

Here is how to write the same algorithm recursively:

```
def factorial(n):
    if n == 0:
        return 1
    return n * factorial(n - 1)
```

First, you define a function called `factorial` that accepts the number, n, as a parameter. Next comes your base case. Your function will call itself repeatedly until n is 0, at which point it will return 1 and will stop calling itself.

```
if n == 0:
    return 1
```

Whenever the base case is not satisfied, this line of code executes:

```
return n * factorial(n - 1)
```

As you can see, your code calls the `factorial` function, which is itself. If this is your first time seeing a recursive algorithm, this probably looks strange to you, and it might even look like this code could not possibly work. But I promise you it does work. In this case, your `factorial` function calls itself and returns the result. However, it does not call itself with the value of n; rather, it calls it with the value of n – 1. Eventually, n will be less than 1, which will satisfy your base case:

```
if n == 0:
    return 1
```

That is all the code you have to write for your recursive algorithm, which is only four lines of code:

```
def factorial(n):
    if n == 0:
        return 1
    return n * factorial(n - 1)
```

So, how does it work? Internally, each time your function hits a return statement, it puts it on a stack. A stack is a type of data structure you will learn more about in Part II. It is like a list in Python, but you remove items in the same order you added them. Let's say you call your recursive factorial function like this:

```
factorial(3)
```

Your variable, n, starts as 3. Your function tests your base case, which is False, so Python executes this line of code:

```
return n * factorial(n - 1)
```

Python does not know the result of n * factorial(n - 1) yet, so it puts it on the stack.

```
# Internal stack (do not try to run this code)

# n = 3
[return n * factorial( n - 1)]
```

Then, your function calls itself again after decrementing n by 1:

```
factorial(2)
```

Your function tests your base case again, which evaluates to False, so Python executes this line of code:

```
return n * factorial(n - 1)
```

Python does not know the result of n * factorial(n – 1) yet, so it puts it on the stack.

```
# Internal stack

# n = 3                          # n = 2
[return n * factorial( n - 1), return n * factorial( n - 1),]
```

Once again, your function calls itself after decrementing n by 1:

```
factorial(1)
```

Python does not know the result of n * factorial(n – 1) yet, so it puts it on the stack.

```
# Internal stack

# n = 3                        # n = 2                        # n = 1
[return n * factorial( n - 1), return n * factorial( n - 1), return n *
factorial( n - 1),]
```

Again, your function calls itself after decrementing n by 1, but this time n is 0, which means your base case is satisfied, so you return 1.

```
if n == 0:
    return 1
```

Python puts the return value on the stack again, but this time it knows what it is returning: the number 1. Now, Python's internal stack looks like this:

```
# Internal stack

# n = 3                        # n = 2                        # n = 1
[return n * factorial( n - 1), return n * factorial( n - 1), return n * factorial(
n - 1), 1]
```

Because Python knows the last return result, it can now calculate the previous return result and remove the previous result from the stack. In other words, Python multiples 1 * n, and n is 1.

```
1 * 1 = 1
```

Now, Python's internal stack looks like this:

```
# Internal stack

# n = 3                        # n = 2
[return n * factorial( n - 1), return n * factorial( n - 1), 1]
```

Once again, because Python knows the last return result, it can calculate the previous return result and remove the previous result from the stack.

```
2 * 1 = 2
```

Now, Python's internal stack looks like this:

```
# Internal stack

# n = 3
[return n * factorial( n - 1), 2]
```

Finally, because Python knows the last return result, it can calculate the previous return result, remove the previous result from the stack, and return the answer.

```
3 * 2 = 6

# Internal stack

[return 6]
```

As you can now see, calculating the factorial of a number is a perfect example of a problem you can solve by finding solutions to smaller instances of the same problem. By recognizing that and writing a recursive algorithm, you created an elegant solution to calculate a number's factorial.

When to Use Recursion

How often you want to use recursion in your algorithms is up to you. Any algorithm you can write recursively, you can also write iteratively. The main advantage of recursion is how elegant it is. As you saw earlier, your iterative solution to calculate factorials took six lines of code, whereas your recursive solution took only four. A disadvantage of recursive algorithms is that they often take up more memory because they have to hold data on Python's internal stack. Recursive functions can also be more difficult than iterative algorithms to read and debug because it can be harder to follow what is happening in a recursive algorithm.

Whether or not you use recursion to solve a problem depends on the specific situation, for example, how important memory usage is versus how much more elegant your recursive algorithm will be than a corresponding iterative algorithm. Later in the book, you will see more examples where recursion offers a more elegant solution than an iterative algorithm, like traversing a binary tree.

Vocabulary

iterative algorithm: An algorithm that solves problems by repeating steps over and over, typically using a loop.

recursion: A method of solving a problem where the solution depends on solutions to smaller instances of the same problem.

base case: A condition that ends a recursive algorithm to stop it from continuing forever.

factorial: The product of all positive integers less than or equal to a number.

Challenge

1. Print the numbers from 1 to 10 recursively.

3

Search Algorithms

An algorithm must be seen to be believed.

Donald Knuth

As a professional programmer, you will spend a lot of time working with data. If you become a web or app developer, you will display data to users when they visit your website or app. Often, you have to manipulate the data before you can show it to them. If you become a data scientist, you will spend even more time working with data. Maybe Netflix will hire you to use its data to improve its algorithm for recommending movies. Or Instagram will employ you to analyze its data to help keep users on its platform longer.

One of the most fundamental things a programmer working with data needs to know is how to search it. Computer scientists search data by writing a **search algorithm**: an algorithm that looks for data in a data set. A **data set** is a collection of data. Two common examples of search algorithms are linear and binary searches. As a professional programmer, you most likely will not spend much time implementing search algorithms because programming languages like Python have them built-in. However, learning how to code a few search algorithms will make you a better programmer because it will help you better understand fundamental computer science concepts such as linear and logarithmic order of magnitudes. It is also crucial for you to understand these algorithms to know which of Python's built-in search algorithms to use and how they will perform on different data sets.

In this chapter, you will learn how to search a list for a number using two different algorithms: a linear search and a binary search. Then, after you code each search algorithm yourself, I will show you how to perform the same search using Python's built-in tools.

Linear Search

In a **linear search**, you iterate through every element in a data set and compare it to the target number. If your comparison finds a match, the number is in the list. If your algorithm ends without finding a match, the number is not in the list.

Here is a linear search algorithm in Python:

```python
def linear_search(a_list, n):
    for i in a_list:
        if i == n:
            return True
    return False

a_list = [1, 8, 32, 91, 5, 15, 9, 100, 3]
print(linear_search(a_list, 91))

>> True
```

The first part of your program calls your `linear_search` function and passes in a list and the number to search for, *n*:

```python
a_list = [1, 8, 32, 91, 5, 15, 9, 100, 3]
print(linear_search(a_list, 91))
```

In this case, *n* is 91, so your algorithm is looking to see if 91 is in `a_list`.
You then use a `for` loop to iterate through each element in `a_list`:

```python
for i in a_list:
```

Next, you use an `if` statement to compare each element in `a_list` to `n`:

```python
if i == n:
```

If there is a match, you return `True`. If you make it through the list and there is no match, you return `False`:

```python
for i in a_list:
    if i == n:
        return True
return False
```

When you run your program, it returns `True` because the number, *n* (in this case, 91), is in `a_list`:

```python
print(linear_search(a_list, 91))

>> True
```

If you rerun your program but search for 1,003 instead of 91, your program will return `False` because 1,003 is not in `a_list`:

```python
print(linear_search(a_list, 1003))

>> False
```

When to Use a Linear Search

A linear search's time complexity is O(n). In the worst-case scenario, in a list of 10 items, your algorithm will take 10 steps. The best-case scenario for a linear search is O(1) because the item you are looking for could be the first item in the list, so your algorithm will take only one step because it stops as soon as it finds a match. On average, a linear search will take *n*/2 steps.

You should consider using a linear search when your data is not sorted. **Sorted data** is data arranged in a meaningful way. For example, you can sort a list of numbers sequentially (either ascending or descending):

```
# Unsorted List
the_list = [12, 19, 13, 15, 14, 10, 18]

# List Sorted in Ascending Order
the_list = [10, 12, 13, 14, 15, 18, 19]
```

If your data is sorted, you can use a more efficient binary search, which you will learn about shortly.

When you are programming in the real world, instead of writing your own linear search, you can use Python's built-in keyword `in`. Here is how to perform a linear search on a list of numbers using Python's `in` keyword:

```
unsorted_list = [1, 45, 4, 32, 3]
print(45 in unsorted_list)

>> True
```

Using Python's `in` keyword, you performed a linear search on `unsorted_list` in just one line of code.

In the examples so far, you've searched only for numbers. You can also use a linear search to find characters in strings. In Python, you can search for a character in a string using a linear search like this:

```
print('a' in 'apple')
```

Binary Search

A **binary search** is another, faster algorithm for searching a list for a number. However, you cannot use a binary search on every data set because it works only when your data is sorted.

A binary search searches for an element in a list by dividing it into halves. Suppose you have the list of numbers shown in Figure 3.1 sorted (from lowest to highest) and you are looking for the number 19.

Figure 3.1: Sorted data set for a binary search

Your first step in a binary search is to locate the middle number. There are seven items in this list, so the middle number is 14 (Figure 3.2).

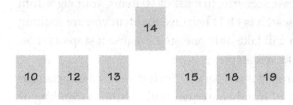

Figure 3.2: A binary search first locates the middle number.

Since 14 is not the number you are searching for, you continue.

The next step is to determine whether the number you are looking for is greater than or less than the middle number. The number you are looking for, 19, is greater than 14, so there is no need to search the bottom half of the list. You can get rid of it. Now all that is left is the upper half of the list with three numbers left to search (Figure 3.3).

Figure 3.3: The next step in a binary search eliminates the half of the data that cannot contain the number.

Next, you repeat the process by locating the middle number again, which is now 18 (Figure 3.4).

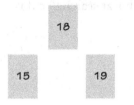

Figure 3.4: A binary search then finds the middle number again.

Since 18 is not the number you are searching for, you again determine whether you keep the lower half or upper half of the list. Because 19 is greater than 18, you keep the upper half and eliminate the lower half.

That leaves only one number, 19, which is the number you are searching for (Figure 3.5). If the number were not 19, you would know it is not in the list.

19

Figure 3.5: Our binary search found our number.

In a linear search, it would have taken seven steps to find 19. It took only three steps with a binary search, which is less than half the number of steps.

Here is how you implement a binary search in Python:

```
def binary_search(a_list, n):
    first = 0
    last = len(a_list) - 1
    while last >= first:
        mid = (first + last) // 2
        if a_list[mid] == n:
            return True
        else:
            if n < a_list[mid]:
                last = mid - 1
            else:
                first = mid + 1
    return False
```

Your function `binary_search` takes two arguments, a_list and n (the target number):

```
def binary_search(a_list, n):
```

You use the variables `first` and `last` to keep track of the beginning and the end of the list you are searching. You start by setting the value of `first` to 0. Next, you assign the variable `last` to the length of the list minus one. You will change the value of these variables as you divide a_list into smaller and smaller segments:

```
first = 0
last = len(a_list) - 1
```

Your algorithm's loop continues as long as there are still items in your list:

```
while last >= first:
```

Inside your loop, you locate the midpoint of a_list by adding `first` plus `last` and then dividing by 2:

```
mid = (first + last) // 2
```

The double-slash is the **floor division operator**, which returns the whole value of division, rounded down. For example, 7 divided by 2 is 3.5, but with floor division, it is 3. You use floor division, so `mid` is always a whole number because indexes are always whole numbers.

Next, you use a conditional statement to check whether the element at the midpoint of your list is the element you are looking for. If it is, you return `True` because you found the number you are looking for:

```
if a_list[mid] == n:
    return True
```

If the item at the midpoint of your list is not the target item, you check whether the target item is greater than or less than the midpoint value. If the target item is less than the midpoint value, you set `last` to the midpoint value minus 1, which cuts off the upper half of the list from further processing:

```
if n < a_list[mid]:
    last = mid - 1
```

If the target item is greater than the midpoint value, you set the value of `first` to the midpoint value plus 1, which cuts off the lower half of the list from further processing:

```
else:
    first = mid + 1
```

Your loop then repeats on a smaller segment of the list you create using the variables `first` and `last`:

```
mid = (first + last) // 2
```

When your loop terminates, your function returns `False` because if you've made it to the end of your function, the number is not in your iterable:

```
return False
```

When to Use a Binary Search

A binary search takes $O(\log n)$ time. It is more efficient than a linear search because you don't have to search an entire list. Instead, you can throw out whole list segments without searching them. A binary search's efficiency makes an enormous difference when you are dealing with large amounts of data. For example, say you are searching a list with a million numbers. If you performed a linear search, it might take you a million steps to complete your search. With a logarithmic binary search, on the other hand, it would take you only 20 steps.

Let's take a closer look at what it means for an algorithm to be logarithmic. **Exponentiation** is a mathematical operation you write as b^n (or b**n in Python), where you multiply a number b times itself n times. In this equation, the number b is called the **base**, and the number n is called the **exponent**. The process of exponentiation means raising b to the power n. For example, 2**2 = 2*2, 2**3 = 2*2*2, and so on. A **logarithm** is the power you must raise a number to in order to produce another number. In other words, it is the inverse of exponentiation. For example, a logarithm can tell you how many times you need to multiply 2 by itself to get 8. That question in mathematical notation is $\log_2(8)$. The solution to $\log_2(8)$ is 3 because you need to multiply 2 by itself 3 times to get 8 (Figure 3.6).

Figure 3.6: Exponential notation versus logarithmic notation

In a binary search, the first time you halve your list, you will have $n/2$ items left in it. After the second iteration, you will have $n/2/2$ items left, and after the third iteration, you will have $n/2/2/2$ items left. Put another way, after your first iteration in a binary search, there will be $n/2*1$ items left, and $n/2**3$ items left after the third iteration. So, more generally, after x iterations, you will have $n/2**x$ items left in your list.

You can use a logarithm to solve how many iterations it will take a binary search to find a number in a list in the worst-case scenario. For example, say you have a list with 100 numbers in it and you want to know how many iterations it will take a binary search to discover a number is not there. To answer this, you need to solve for n in $2**n = 100$, which is the same as $\log_2(100)$. You can solve this equation intuitively by guessing. For example, you might start by guessing that n is 5, but $2**5$ is 32, which is too small. You can keep guessing: $2**6$ is 64, which is also too small, and $2**7$ is 128, which is greater than 100, and is thus your answer. In other words, if you perform a binary search on a list with 100 items, and the item is not there, it will take your algorithm 7 steps to determine that. In other words, $100/2/2/2/2/2/2/2 < 1$.

When you run a binary search, it divides your list in half each iteration, which means the logarithm describing its run time is base 2. However, in big O notation, a logarithm's base doesn't matter because you can change it by multiplying the logarithm by a constant. The math details are beyond the scope of this book, but the important thing to know is that the logarithm base doesn't matter in big O notation. What is important is whether an algorithm is logarithmic, which usually happens when your algorithm reduces the computation amount by half or some other significant amount each iteration.

Because of how efficient a binary search is, if you have sorted data you need to search, it is usually best to use one. However, even if you have unsorted data, sometimes it is worth sorting it to take advantage of a binary search. For example, if you have a large list and plan to do many searches, it might benefit you to sort your data once to vastly speed up each one of the searches you will do in the future.

As with a linear search, Python has a built-in module to perform a binary search, which you should use when writing real-world applications. The key to writing a binary search using Python's built-in tools is to use `bisect_left` from the `bisect` module, which finds the index of an existing element in a sorted list using a binary search:

```
from bisect import bisect_left


sorted_fruits = ['apple', 'banana', 'orange', 'plum']
bisect_left(sorted_fruits, 'banana')

>> 1
```

In this case, `bisect_left` returned 1 because `'banana'` is at index 1 in `sorted_fruits`. If the item you are looking for is not in your sorted iterable, `bisect_left` returns where it would be if it were there.

```
from bisect import bisect_left


sorted_fruits = ['apple', 'banana', 'orange', 'plum']
bisect_left(sorted_fruits, 'kiwi')

>> 2
```

As you can see, `'kiwi'` is not in your sorted iterable, but if it were, it would be at index 2.

Because `bisect_left` tells you where an item should go if it isn't there, to check if an item is in an iterable, you need to see if the index is within the iterable (`bisect` could return a position outside of your iterable) and if the item at the index `bisect_left` returns is the value you are looking for. Here is how to use `bisect_left` to perform a binary search in Python:

```
from bisect import bisect_left


def binary_search(an_iterable, target):
    index = bisect_left(an_iterable, target)
    if index <= len(an_iterable) and an_iterable[index] == target:
        return True
    return False
```

If `bisect_left` returns an index within your iterable and that index contains your target, you return `True` because the item is in your iterable. Otherwise, it is not, and you return `False`.

Searching for Characters

You know how to search for characters in a list using Python's built-in linear and binary search tools. But what if you had to write a linear or binary search from scratch to search for characters instead of numbers? To understand how to search for characters, you need to understand more about how a computer stores them.

A **character set** is a map between characters and binary numbers. Computer scientists use character encoding to implement different character sets. In American Standard Code for Information Interchange (ASCII), your computer maps each letter of the alphabet to a seven-bit number. Figure 3.7 shows the relationship between binary and the different characters in the English language.

For example, the ASCII value of *A* is 1000001 in binary (you will learn more about binary later in the book) and 65 in base 10 (the number system you use every day). The binary digit for *b* is 01100010. Uppercase letters, lowercase letters, punctuation symbols, numerals, and various control characters that indicate actions, such as page breaks and line feeds, all have ASCII codes. There are ASCII codes

Dec	Bin	Char	Dec	Bin	Char	Dec	Bin	Char	Dec	Bin	Char
0	0000 0000	[NUL]	32	0010 0000	space	64	0100 0000	@	96	0110 0000	`
1	0000 0001	[SOH]	33	0010 0001	!	65	0100 0001	A	97	0110 0001	a
2	0000 0010	[STX]	34	0010 0010	"	66	0100 0010	B	98	0110 0010	b
3	0000 0011	[ETX]	35	0010 0011	#	67	0100 0011	C	99	0110 0011	c
4	0000 0100	[EOT]	36	0010 0100	$	68	0100 0100	D	100	0110 0100	d
5	0000 0101	[ENQ]	37	0010 0101	%	69	0100 0101	E	101	0110 0101	e
6	0000 0110	[ACK]	38	0010 0110	&	70	0100 0110	F	102	0110 0110	f
7	0000 0111	[BEL]	39	0010 0111	'	71	0100 0111	G	103	0110 0111	g
8	0000 1000	[BS]	40	0010 1000	(	72	0100 1000	H	104	0110 1000	h
9	0000 1001	[TAB]	41	0010 1001	)	73	0100 1001	I	105	0110 1001	i
10	0000 1010	[LF]	42	0010 1010	*	74	0100 1010	J	106	0110 1010	j
11	0000 1011	[VT]	43	0010 1011	+	75	0100 1011	K	107	0110 1011	k
12	0000 1100	[FF]	44	0010 1100	,	76	0100 1100	L	108	0110 1100	l
13	0000 1101	[CR]	45	0010 1101	-	77	0100 1101	M	109	0110 1101	m
14	0000 1110	[SO]	46	0010 1110	.	78	0100 1110	N	110	0110 1110	n
15	0000 1111	[SI]	47	0010 1111	/	79	0100 1111	O	111	0110 1111	o
16	0001 0000	[DLE]	48	0011 0000	0	80	0101 0000	P	112	0111 0000	p
17	0001 0001	[DC1]	49	0011 0001	1	81	0101 0001	Q	113	0111 0001	q
18	0001 0010	[DC2]	50	0011 0010	2	82	0101 0010	R	114	0111 0010	r
19	0001 0011	[DC3]	51	0011 0011	3	83	0101 0011	S	115	0111 0011	s
20	0001 0100	[DC4]	52	0011 0100	4	84	0101 0100	T	116	0111 0100	t
21	0001 0101	[NAK]	53	0011 0101	5	85	0101 0101	U	117	0111 0101	u
22	0001 0110	[SYN]	54	0011 0110	6	86	0101 0110	V	118	0111 0110	v
23	0001 0111	[ETB]	55	0011 0111	7	87	0101 0111	W	119	0111 0111	w
24	0001 1000	[CAN]	56	0011 1000	8	88	0101 1000	X	120	0111 1000	x
25	0001 1001	[EM]	57	0011 1001	9	89	0101 1001	Y	121	0111 1001	y
26	0001 1010	[SUB]	58	0011 1010	:	90	0101 1010	Z	122	0111 1010	z
27	0001 1011	[ESC]	59	0011 1011	;	91	0101 1011	[	123	0111 1011	{
28	0001 1100	[FS]	60	0011 1100	<	92	0101 1100	\	124	0111 1100		
29	0001 1101	[GS]	61	0011 1101	=	93	0101 1101	]	125	0111 1101	}
30	0001 1110	[RS]	62	0011 1110	>	94	0101 1110	^	126	0111 1110	~
31	0001 1111	[US]	63	0011 1111	?	95	0101 1111	_	127	0111 1111	[DEL]

Figure 3.7: ASCII chart

for the numbers 0 through 9 because 0 through 9 in the ASCII table are not numeric values. They are characters for nonmathematical purposes, such as expressing the numerals in the street address 26 Broadway Street, New York. Because ASCII maps each character to a 7-bit binary number, it can only represent a maximum of 128 different characters (2^7 is 128). Most computers, however, extend ASCII to 8 bits so that it can represent 256 characters.

While you can represent the 256 characters in the Latin-script alphabet with ASCII, it does not support enough characters to deal with the text from other writing systems, such as Japanese or Mandarin. To deal with this problem, computer scientists developed the **Unicode** character set. **Character encoding** means assigning a number to characters for digital representation. UTF-8 is one of the character encoding methods computer scientists use to implement the Unicode character set.

Instead of using 7 or 8 bits like ASCII, UTF-8 uses up to 32 bits to encode each character, which allows you to represent more than a million characters. UTF-8 is compatible with ASCII because it uses the same bit representation for the Latin-script alphabet. For example, both ASCII and UTF-8 represent an uppercase A with 1000001.

You can use Python's built-in `ord()` function to get a character's ASCII value:

```
print(ord('a'))

>> 97
```

As you can see, the ASCII value for *a* is 97 (in base 10).

The `ord()` function is useful when you need to work directly with the underlying ASCII codes of different characters. To modify the binary search you wrote earlier to search for characters, you have to get and compare the ASCII values of characters. Each time through your loop, you check to see whether the ASCII code of each character is higher than, lower than, or equal to the character's ASCII code you are looking for. Instead of showing you the solution here, I challenge you to code it yourself at the end of this chapter.

You now know how linear and binary searches work and when to use them when you are searching for data. While a binary search is very efficient, it is not the fastest way to search for data. In Part II, you will learn how to search for data using a hash table and why it is the most efficient kind of search.

Vocabulary

search algorithm: An algorithm that looks for data in a data set.

data set: A collection of data.

linear search: A search algorithm that iterates through each element in a set of data and compares it to the target number.

sorted data: Data arranged in a meaningful way.

binary search: Another algorithm for searching a list for a number, and it is faster than a linear search.

floor division operator: An operator that returns the whole value of division, rounded down.

exponentiation: A mathematical operation you write as b^n (or `b**n` in Python), where you multiply a number b times itself n times.

base: The b in the equation for exponentiation (b^n).

exponent: The n in the equation for exponentiation (b^n).

logarithm: The power you must raise a number to in order to produce another number.

character set: A map between characters and binary numbers.

ASCII: The American Standard Code for Information Interchange character set.

Unicode: A character set that can store more characters than ASCII.

character encoding: Assigning a number to characters for digital representation.

UTF-8: One of the methods of character encoding computer scientists use to implement the Unicode character set.

Challenge

1. Given a list of words in alphabetical order, write a function that performs a binary search for a word and returns whether it is in the list.

4 Sorting Algorithms

I think the bubble sort would be the wrong way to go.

Barack Obama

As a computer scientist, in addition to searching for data, you will often have to sort data. **Sorting data** means arranging it in a meaningful way. For example, if you have a list of numbers, you could sort them from the smallest to the largest (ascending). Or, imagine you are building an app that keeps track of the books each user has read. In an app like this, you might want to allow the user to see their books sorted in different ways. For example, you could give them the option to see their books sorted from the shortest book to the longest, oldest to newest, or newest to oldest.

There are many different sorting algorithms to help you sort data, each with strengths and weaknesses. For example, some sort algorithms work best in specific situations, like if an iterable is nearly sorted. In this chapter, you will learn about bubble sort, insertion sort, and merge sort. Other popular sorts include quicksort, shell sort, and heap sort. There are many sorting algorithms you will have to use in only rare circumstances, so after teaching you a few sorts, I spend the remainder of the chapter showing you how to use Python's built-in functions to sort data, something you will often use in real-world programming.

When you are building your programs in the real world, you should almost always use your programming language's built-in sorting function. You should not implement the classic sorting algorithms discussed here (except in rare circumstances) because modern programming languages like Python have built-in sorting functions that are faster. However, learning a few of the classic sorting algorithms will help you better understand time complexity and teach you concepts you can use in situations other than sorting, such as the merge step in a merge sort.

Bubble Sort

Bubble sort is a sorting algorithm where you iterate through a list of numbers, compare each number to the next number, and swap them if they are out of order. Computer scientists call it a bubble sort because the numbers with the highest values "bubble up" to the end of the list, and the numbers with the smallest values move to the beginning of the list as the algorithm progresses.

Say you have the following list:

```
[32, 1, 9, 6]
```

First, you compare 1 and 32:

```
[32, 1, 9, 6]
```

Thirty-two is bigger, so you swap them:

```
[1, 32, 9, 6]
```

Next, you compare 32 and 9:

```
[1, 32, 9, 6]
```

Thirty-two is larger, so you swap them again:

```
[1, 9, 32, 6]
```

Finally, you compare 32 and 6:

```
[1, 9, 32, 6]
```

Once again, you swap them:

```
[1, 9, 6, 32]
```

As you can see, 32 "bubbled up" to the end of the list. However, your list is still not in order because 9 and 6 are not in the right spots. So, your algorithm starts at the beginning again and compares 1 and 9:

```
[1, 9, 6, 32]
```

Nothing happens because 1 is not greater than 9. Next, it compares 9 and 6:

```
[1, 9, 6, 32]
```

Nine is greater than 6, so you swap them, and your list is now in order:

```
[1, 6, 9, 32]
```

In a bubble sort, the largest number in your list will move to the end of your list at the end of your algorithm's first iteration, but if the smallest number in your list starts at the end, it will take multiple passes for your algorithm to move it to the beginning of your list. For instance, in this example, 32 ended up at the end of your list after one iteration. Say your list started like this, though:

```
[32, 6, 9, 1]
```

In this case, it will take four iterations to move 1 from the end of the list to the beginning.

It can be helpful to use a bubble sort visualizer to better understand how this algorithm works. There are many bubble sort visualizers you can search for on the internet that can cement your understanding of how this sorting algorithm works. I recommend doing this for the sorting algorithms you will learn about in this chapter.

Here is how to write a bubble sort algorithm in Python:

```python
def bubble_sort(a_list):
    list_length = len(a_list) - 1
    for i in range(list_length):
        for j in range(list_length):
            if a_list[j] > a_list[j + 1]:
                a_list[j], a_list[j + 1] = a_list[j + 1], a_list[j]
    return a_list
```

Your function `bubble_sort` takes a list of numbers, called `a_list`, as a parameter:

```python
def bubble_sort(a_list):
```

Inside your function, you get your list's length, subtract 1, and save the result in `list_length` to control how many iterations your algorithm will make:

```python
list_length = len(a_list) - 1
```

Your function has two nested loops so that you can iterate through your list and make comparisons:

```python
for i in range(list_length):
    for j in range(list_length)
```

Inside your inner `for` loop, you use an `if` statement to compare the current number to the one after it by adding 1 to the current number's index:

```python
if a_list[j] > a_list[j + 1]:
```

This line of code is the current number:

```python
a_list[j]
```

This line of code is the next number in your list:

```python
a_list[j + 1]
```

If the current number is greater than the next number, you swap them. The following Python syntax allows you to swap two items without loading one of the items into a temporary variable:

```python
a_list[j], a_list[j + 1] = a_list[j + 1], a_list[j]
```

Your algorithm's comparisons all happen inside your inner loop. Your outer loop is there only to keep your algorithm running for as many swaps as it takes to put your list in order. Take, for example, the list from the beginning of the section:

```python
[32, 1, 9, 6]
```

After one inner-loop iteration, your list looks like this:

```python
[1, 9, 6, 32]
```

Recall, however, that this list is not in order. If you had only your inner loop, your algorithm would end prematurely, and your list would not be in order. That is why you need your outer loop: to start your algorithm's inner loop over from the beginning and repeat it until your list is in order.

You can improve the efficiency of your bubble sort by including − i in your second `for` loop. That way, your inner loop will not compare the last two numbers the first time through the loop; the second time through the loop, it will not compare the last three numbers; and so on.

```
def bubble_sort(a_list):
    list_length = len(a_list) - 1
    for i in range(list_length):
        for j in range(list_length - i):
            if a_list[j] > a_list[j + 1]:
                a_list[j], a_list[j + 1] = a_list[j + 1], a_list[j]
    return a_list
```

You don't have to make these comparisons because the highest numbers bubble to the end of your list. For instance, in the initial example at the beginning of this section, you saw 32 bubbled up to the end of your list after the first iteration of your sort. That means the largest number is at the end of your list after the first iteration; the second largest number is at the next-to-the-last spot after the second iteration, and so forth. This means you do not need to compare the other numbers to them and can end your loop early. For example, take a look at the list from the beginning of this section:

```
[32, 1, 9, 6]
```

After one full inner-loop iteration, it looks like this:

```
[1, 9, 6, 32]
```

After one iteration, the largest number moves to the end of your list, so you no longer have to compare numbers to 32 because you know it is the largest number in your list.

The second time through your inner loop, the second-largest value will move to its final position, second from the end, etc.

```
[1, 6, 9, 32]
```

So, each time through your inner loop, your inner loop can terminate sooner.

You can also make your bubble sort more efficient by adding a variable that keeps track of whether your algorithm made any swaps in your inner loop. If you get through an inner loop with no swaps, your list is sorted, and you can exit the loop and return your list without any further processing.

```
def bubble_sort(a_list):
    list_length = len(a_list) - 1
    for i in range(list_length):
        no_swaps = True
        for j in range(list_length - i):
            if a_list[j] > a_list[j + 1]:
                a_list[j], a_list[j + 1] = a_list[j + 1], a_list[j]
```

```
                no_swaps = False
        if no_swaps:
            return a_list
    return a_list
```

In this case, you added a variable called `no_swaps` that starts as `True` at the beginning of your inner loop. If you swap two numbers inside your inner loop, you set it to `False`. If you make it through your inner loop and `no_swaps` is `True`, your list is sorted, and you can end your algorithm. This small change makes your bubble sort run significantly faster when a list starts nearly sorted.

When to Use Bubble Sort

In this implementation of bubble sort, your algorithm sorts numbers, but you can also write a bubble sort (or any other sort) that sorts strings. For example, you could modify a bubble sort to sort strings alphabetically by each word's first letter.

A bubble sort's main advantage is how simple it is to implement, making it a good starting point for teaching sorting algorithms. Because a bubble sort relies on two nested `for` loops, its time complexity is $O(n**2)$, which means while it can be acceptable for small sets of data, it is not an efficient choice for larger data sets.

A bubble sort is also stable. A **stable sort** is one that does not disturb any sequences other than the one specified by the sort key. For example, say you have a database containing records for these four animals:

Akita

Bear

Tiger

Albatross

If you sort by the first letter of the first character, you expect this output:

Stable Sort

Akita

Albatross

Bear

Tiger

This output is an example of a stable sort because Akita and Albatross are in the same order as in the original list, even though your sort looked only at the first letter of each name. An unstable sort might disrupt the original order of the two animal names that start with *A*, so Albatross might come before Akita even though Akita came before Albatross in the original list.

Unstable Sort

Albatross

Akita

Bear

Tiger

In other words, in a stable sort, when there are two equal keys, the items maintain their original order.

Despite its stability, because a bubble sort is O(n**2) and because there are other, more efficient sorts you can use (which you are about to learn), you are unlikely to see anyone using a bubble sort outside of the classroom.

Insertion Sort

An **insertion sort** is a sorting algorithm where you sort data like you sort a deck of cards. First, you split a list of numbers into two: a sorted left half and an unsorted right half. Then, you sort the left half the same way you sort a hand of playing cards. For example, when you sort a hand of five cards in ascending order, you go through your cards one by one, inserting each card to the right of every card lower than it.

Here is how an insertion sort algorithm works on a list with four elements: 6, 5, 8, and 2. Your algorithm starts with the second item in your list, which is 5:

```
[6, 5, 8, 2]
```

Next, you compare the current item to the previous item in your list. Six is greater than 5, so you swap them:

```
[5, 6, 8, 2]
```

Now the left half of your list is sorted, but the right half is not:

```
[5, 6, 8, 2]
```

Then, you move to the third item in your list. Six is not greater than 8, so you don't swap 8 and 6:

```
[5, 6, 8, 2]
```

Because the left half of your list is sorted, you do not have to compare 8 and 5:

```
[5, 6, 8, 2]
```

Next, you compare 8 and 2:

```
[5, 6, 8, 2]
```

Because 8 is greater than 2, you go one by one through the sorted left half of the list, comparing 2 to each number until it arrives at the front and the entire list is sorted:

```
[2, 5, 6, 8]
```

Here is how to code an insertion sort in Python:

```
def insertion_sort(a_list):
    for i in range(1, len(a_list)):
        value = a_list[i]
        while i > 0 and a_list[i - 1] > value:
            a_list[i] = a_list[i - 1]
            i = i - 1
        a_list[i] = value
    return a_list
```

You start by defining an `insertion_sort` function that takes a list of numbers as input:

```
def insertion_sort(a_list):
```

Your function uses a `for` loop to iterate through each item in the list. Then it uses a `while` loop for the comparisons your algorithm makes when adding a new number to the sorted left side of your list:

```
for i in range(1, len(a_list)):
    ...
    while i > 0 and a_list[i - 1] > value:
        ...
```

Your `for` loop begins with the second item in your list (index 1). Inside your loop, you keep track of the current number in the variable `value`:

```
for i in range(1, len(a_list)):
    value = a_list[i]
```

Your `while` loop moves items from the unsorted right half of your list to the sorted left half. It continues as long as two things are true: `i` must be greater than 0, and the previous item in the list must be greater than the item that comes after it. The variable `i` must be greater than 0 because your `while` loop compares two numbers, and if `i` is 0, that means your algorithm is at the first item in the list, and there is no previous number to compare it to.

```
while i > 0 and a_list[i - 1] > value:
```

Your `while` loop executes only if the number in `value` is smaller than the previous item in the list. Inside your `while` loop, you move the greater value to the right of your list. Then, your algorithm works on finding out where to put the smaller value in the sorted left half of your list. You decrement `i` so your loop can make another comparison and see if the smaller number needs to move even farther to the left.

```
while i > 0 and a_list[i - 1] > value:
    a_list[i] = a_list[i - 1]
    i = i - 1
```

When your `while` loop terminates, you insert the current number in `value` in the correct position in the sorted left half of the list:

```
a_list[i] = value
```

Let's take a look at how your insertion sort algorithm works with the following list:

```
[6, 5, 8, 2]
```

The first time through your `for` loop, `i` is 1, and `value` is 5:

```
for i in range(1, len(a_list)):
    value = a_list[i]
```

The following code in bold is `True` because `i > 0` and `6 > 5`, so your `while` loop executes:

```
while i > 0 and a_list[i - 1] > value:
    a_list[i] = a_list[i - 1]
    i = i - 1
a_list[i] = value
```

This code:

```
while i > 0 and a_list[i - 1] > value:
    a_list[i] = a_list[i - 1]
    i = i - 1
a_list[i] = value
```

changes your list from this:

```
[6, 5, 8, 2]
```

to this:

```
[6, 6, 8, 2]
```

And this code:

```
while i > 0 and a_list[i - 1] > value:
    a_list[i] = a_list[i - 1]
    i = i - 1
a_list[i] = value
```

decrements `i` by 1. The variable `i` is now 0, which means your `while` loop will not execute again:

```
while i > 0 and a_list[i - 1] > value:
    a_list[i] = a_list[i - 1]
    i = i - 1
a_list[i] = value
```

Next, this line of code:

```
while i > 0 and a_list[i - 1] > value:
    a_list[i] = a_list[i - 1]
    i = i - 1
a_list[i] = value
```

changes your list from this:

```
[6, 6, 8, 2]
```

to this:

```
[5, 6, 8, 2]
```

You've sorted the first two items in your list, and all your algorithm has to do now is repeat the same process to sort the right half of the list containing 8 and 2.

When to Use Insertion Sort

Like a bubble sort, an insertion sort is stable. Also like a bubble sort, an insertion sort is $O(n**2)$, so it is not very efficient. However, unlike a bubble sort, computer scientists use insertion sorts in real-world applications. For example, an insertion sort may be an efficient choice if you have nearly sorted data. When a list is sorted or almost sorted, an insertion sort's time complexity is $O(n)$, which is very efficient.

Say you have the following list:

```
[1, 2, 3, 4, 5, 7, 6]
```

As you can see, all the numbers are sorted except for the last two numbers. Because the second loop (the `while` loop) in an insertion sort executes only if two numbers are out of order, sorting this nearly sorted list with an insertion sort takes only eight steps, which is linear because the second loop has to run only once.

Merge Sort

A **merge sort** is a recursive sorting algorithm that continually splits a list in half until there are one or more lists containing one item and then puts them back together in the correct order. Here is how it works. First, you use recursion to continually break your list in half until your original list becomes one or more sublists containing only one number (Figure 4.1).

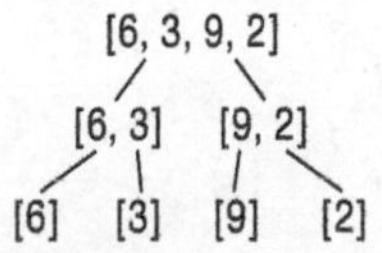

```
        [6, 3, 9, 2]
        /         \
    [6, 3]       [9, 2]
    /    \       /    \
  [6]   [3]    [9]    [2]
```

Figure 4.1: The first part of a merge sort

Lists containing one item are sorted by definition. Once you have sorted lists containing one item each, you merge your sublists two at a time by comparing the first item in each list. Merging your lists means combining them in sorted order.

First, you merge [6] and [3], then you merge [9] and [2]. In this case, each list contains only one number, so you compare the two numbers and put the smallest number at the beginning of your new, merged list and the larger number at the end. Now, you have two sorted lists:

```
[3, 6], [2, 9]
```

Then, you merge these two lists:

```
# unmerged
[3, 6], [2, 9]

#merged
[]
```

First, you compare 3 and 2. Since 2 is smaller, it goes into your merged list:

```
# unmerged
[3, 6], [9]

#merged
[2]
```

Now you compare 3 and 9. Since 3 is smaller, it goes into your merged list:

```
# unmerged
[6], [9]

#merged
[2, 3]
```

Finally, you compare 6 and 9. Since 6 is smaller, it goes into your merged list. Then, you put the 9 into the merged list:

```
# unmerged
[], []

#merged
[2, 3, 6, 9]
```

Now that you've finished all your merges, you have a single, sorted list.

Here is how to implement a merge sort in Python:

```
def merge_sort(a_list):
    if len(a_list) > 1:
```

```
        mid = len(a_list) // 2
        left_half = a_list[:mid]
        right_half = a_list[mid:]
        merge_sort(left_half)
        merge_sort(right_half)

        left_ind = 0
        right_ind = 0
        alist_ind = 0
        while left_ind < len(left_half) and right_ind < len(right_half):
            if left_half[left_ind] <= right_half[right_ind]:
                a_list[alist_ind] = left_half[left_ind]
                left_ind += 1
            else:
                a_list[alist_ind] = right_half[right_ind]
                right_ind += 1
            alist_ind += 1

        while left_ind < len(left_half):
            a_list[alist_ind]=left_half[left_ind]
            left_ind += 1
            alist_ind += 1

        while right_ind < len(right_half):
            a_list[alist_ind]= right_half[right_ind]
            right_ind += 1
            alist_ind += 1
```

This part of your algorithm is responsible for breaking your lists into sublists:

```
if len(a_list) > 1:
    mid = len(a_list) // 2
    left_half = a_list[:mid]
    right_half = a_list[mid:]
    merge_sort(left_half)
    merge_sort(right_half)

    left_ind = 0
    right_ind = 0
    alist_ind = 0
```

This part is responsible for merging two lists:

```
    left_ind = 0
    right_ind = 0
    alist_ind = 0
    while left_ind < len(left_half) and right_ind < len(right_half):
        if left_half[left_ind] <= right_half[right_ind]:
            a_list[alist_ind] = left_half[left_ind]
```

```
            left_ind += 1
        else:
            a_list[alist_ind] = right_half[right_ind]
            right_ind += 1
        alist_ind += 1

    while left_ind < len(left_half):
        a_list[alist_ind]=left_half[left_ind]
        left_ind += 1
        alist_ind += 1

    while right_ind < len(right_half):
        a_list[alist_ind]= right_half[right_ind]
        right_ind += 1
        alist_ind += 1
```

Recursion is the key to this algorithm. We will discuss later in the chapter how the second half of the algorithm that merges lists works. Let's walk through the recursive part function call by call. Say you start with the list from the beginning of this section:

```
[6, 3, 9, 2]
```

The first time you call your merge_sort function, your function creates three variables:

```
# Function call 1

a_list = [6, 3, 9, 2]
left_half = [6, 3]
right_half = [9, 2]
```

You pass a_list to your function, and this code creates the other two variables by dividing a_list into a left half and a right half:

```
mid = len(a_list) // 2
left_half = a_list[:mid]
right_half = a_list[mid:]
```

Next, your function recursively calls itself and passes in left_half as a parameter:

```
merge_sort(left_half)
```

Now, Python creates three more variables:

```
# Function call 2

a_list = [6, 3]
left_half = [6]
right_half = [3]
```

The crucial thing to understand is `left_half` in the first function call and `a_list` in the second function call *point to the same list*. That means when you change `left_half` in the second function call, it changes `a_list` in the first function call.

Now your code calls itself again, but this time `left_half` is [6], and your base case stops further recursion.

```
if len(a_list) > 1:
```

So, Python moves on to the next line of code:

```
merge_sort(right_half)
```

The variable `right_half` is [3], so your base case stops your function from calling itself again.

```
if len(a_list) > 1:
```

Now Python calls your merge code. Your merge code merges `left_half`, which is [6], and `right_half`, which is [3], and saves the result by modifying `a_list`, which is now sorted:

```
# Function call 2

a_list = [3, 6]
left_half = [6]
right_half = [3]
```

As you learned earlier, when you modify `a_list` in function call 2, you are also changing the variable `left_half` in function call 1.

Originally, Python's state during function call 1 looked like this:

```
# Function call 1

a_list = [6, 3, 9, 2]
left_half = [6, 3]
right_half = [9, 2]
```

But in function call 2, you modified `a_list`, which also changed `left_half` in function call 1. Now function call 1's state looks like this:

```
# Function call 1

a_list = [3, 6, 9, 2]
left_half = [3, 6]
right_half = [9, 2]
```

This change is important, because as you know, when you use recursion, Python returns to previous states when you hit your base case. As you can see, `left_half` is now sorted.

Your algorithm then calls itself recursively again, the same process plays out, and `right_half` gets sorted. That means function one's state now looks like this:

```
# Function call 1

a_list = [3, 6, 9, 2]
left_half = [3, 6]
right_half = [2, 9]
```

As you can see, `right_half` is now sorted in function one call's state. Now, when your algorithm comes back to function one's state, it merges `left_half` and `right_half`, which previous recursive function calls have already sorted. So, when your algorithm gets to this point and calls its merge code, your function has two sorted lists, `left_half` and `right_half`, and it just has to merge them to produce your final, sorted list.

Now, let's look at the code that merges two lists. Your merge code starts with three variables, which you set to 0:

```
left_ind = 0
right_ind = 0
alist_ind = 0
```

You use these variables to track the indexes of three lists: `left_half`, `right_half`, and `a_list`.

This code compares each first item in `left_half` to each first item in `right_half` and puts the smaller number in its correct position in `a_list`:

```
while left_ind < len(left_half) and right_ind < len(right_half):
    if left_half[left_ind] <= right_half[right_ind]:
        a_list[alist_ind] = left_half[left_ind]
        left_ind += 1
    else:
        a_list[alist_ind] = right_half[right_ind]
        right_ind += 1
    alist_ind += 1
```

And this code finishes each merge and can also handle a situation in which the two lists you are merging are uneven:

```
while left_ind < len(left_half):
    a_list[alist_ind] = left_half[left_ind]
    left_ind += 1
    alist_ind += 1

while right_ind < len(right_half):
    a_list[alist_ind]= right_half[right_ind]
    right_ind += 1
    alist_ind += 1
```

For example, say you were merging these two lists:

```
[2], [6, 4]
```

Python would call your merge code with these variables:

```
left_ind = 0
right_ind = 0
alist_ind = 0

a_list = [6, 3]
left_half = [6]
right_half = [3]
```

The expressions left_ind < len(left_half) and right_ind < len(right_half) evaluate to True, so you enter your while loop. This code:

```
left_half[left_ind] <= right_half[right_ind]:
```

evaluates to 6 <= 3, which is False, so this code runs:

```
if left_half[left_ind] <= right_half[right_ind]:
    a_list[alist_ind] = left_half[left_ind]
    left_ind += 1
else:
    a_list[alist_ind] = right_half[right_ind]
    right_ind += 1
alist_ind += 1
```

Now your variables look like this:

```
left_ind = 0
right_ind = 1
alist_ind = 1

a_list = [3, 3]
left_half = [6]
right_half = [3]
```

The next time through your while loop, the following code does not execute because right_ind is not less than the length of right_half:

```
while left_ind < len(left_half) and right_ind < len(right_half):
    if left_half[left_ind] <= right_half[right_ind]:
        a_list[alist_ind] = left_half[left_ind]
        left_ind += 1
    else:
        a_list[alist_ind] = right_half[right_ind]
        right_ind += 1
    alist_ind += 1
```

Next, this code executes because `left_ind` is less than the length of `left_half`:

```
while left_ind < len(left_half):
    a_list[alist_ind] = left_half[left_ind]
    left_ind += 1
    alist_ind += 1

while right_ind < len(right_half):
    a_list[alist_ind]= right_half[right_ind]
    right_ind += 1
    alist_ind += 1
```

Now your variables look like this:

```
left_ind = 1
right_ind = 1
alist_ind = 2

a_list = [3, 6]
left_half = [6]
right_half = [3]
```

Your list is now sorted, and your merge is complete.

When to Use Merge Sort

A merge sort is an example of a divide-and-conquer algorithm. A **divide-and-conquer algorithm** is one that recursively breaks a problem into two or more related subproblems until they are simple enough to solve easily. In a merge sort, you break down a list into sublists until each sublist has only one item, making it simple to solve because a list with one item is sorted by definition. A merge sort's run time is $O(n * \log n)$ because while splitting the initial list into sublists is logarithmic, the algorithm requires linear time to handle each item in the sublists as it merges them. With log-linear time complexity, a merge sort is one of the most efficient sorting algorithms and widely used by computer scientists. For example, Python uses merge sort in its built-in sorting algorithms, which you will learn about shortly. Like bubble sort and insertion sort, a merge sort is also stable.

You can also apply the merge concept from a merge sort to situations other than sorting. For example, imagine you are in a classroom with 50 students. Every student has a random amount of change in their pocket, up to $1. What is the best way to add up all of the change? The first answer you may think of is to have the professor walk up to every student and ask them how much change they have and add it all up. That solution is a linear search, and its run time is $O(n)$. Instead of performing a linear search, it is more efficient to have the students merge themselves. Here is how it works: every student will pick the student next to them, take their change, and add it to theirs (and remember the new total). The students without any change then leave the room. You then repeat this process until there is only one student left and they've added up all of the change in the room. Instead of 50 steps, using a merge to count the room's change takes only 6 steps.

Sorting Algorithms in Python

Python has two built-in sort functions: `sorted` and `sort`. Python's sorting functions use Timsort, a hybrid sorting algorithm that combines merge sort and insertion sort. A **hybrid sorting algorithm** is one that combines two or more other algorithms that solve the same problem, either choosing one (depending on the data) or switching between them throughout the algorithm. Timsort's mix of insertion and merge sort makes it an efficient algorithm and is the reason you usually use Python's built-in sorting algorithms instead of trying to code your own.

Python's `sorted` function allows you to sort any iterable, as long as Python can compare the data in it. For example, you can call `sorted` on a list of integers, and Python will return a new list with the integers from the original list sorted in ascending order:

```
a_list = [1, 8, 10, 33, 4, 103]
print(sorted(a_list))

>> [1, 4, 8, 10, 33, 103]
```

If you call `sorted` on a list of strings, Python will return a new list sorted alphabetically by each string's first letter:

```
a_list = ["Guido van Rossum", "James Gosling", "Brendan Eich", "Yukihiro Matsumoto"]
print(sorted(a_list))

>> ['Brendan Eich', 'Guido van Rossum', 'James Gosling', 'Yukihiro Matsumoto']
```

Python's `sorted` function has an optional parameter called `reverse`, so if you want to sort your iterable in descending order, you can pass in `reverse=True`:

```
a_list = [1, 8, 10, 33, 4, 103]
print(sorted(a_list, reverse=True))

>> [103, 33, 10, 8, 4, 1]
```

`Sorted` also has a parameter called `key` that lets you pass in a function. Python then calls that function on each item in your iterable and uses the result to sort it. For example, you can pass in the `len` function, which will sort a list of strings by length:

```
a_list = ["onehundred", "five", "seventy", "two"]
print(sorted(a_list, key=len))

>> ['two', 'five', 'seventy', 'onehundred']
```

Python's other function for sorting is `sort`, which has the same optional parameters as `sorted`, but unlike `sorted`, `sort` works only on lists. Also, unlike `sorted`, `sort` sorts in place: it changes the original list instead of returning a new one. Here is an example of using `sort` on a list:

```
a_list = [1, 8, 10, 33, 4, 103]
a_list.sort()
print(a_list)

>> [1, 4, 8, 10, 33, 103]
```

As you can see, Python sorted the numbers in your original list in ascending order.

Vocabulary

sorting data: Arranging data in a meaningful way.

bubble sort: A sorting algorithm where you iterate through a list of numbers, compare each number with the next number, and swap them if they are out of order.

stable sort: A sort that does not disturb any sequences other than the one specified by the sort key.

insertion sort: A sorting algorithm where you sort data like you sort a deck of cards.

merge sort: A recursive sorting algorithm that continually splits a list in half until there are one or more lists containing one item, and then puts them back together in the correct order.

divide-and-conquer algorithm: An algorithm that recursively breaks a problem into two or more related subproblems until they are simple enough to solve easily.

hybrid sorting algorithm: An algorithm that combines two or more other algorithms that solve the same problem, either choosing one (depending on the data) or switching between them throughout the algorithm.

Challenge

1. Research and write a sorting algorithm that is not a bubble sort, insertion sort, or merge sort.

5 String Algorithms

One of the most important skills any entrepreneur should learn is to program a computer. This is a critical skill if you want to start a tech startup, but a basic knowledge of code is useful even in traditional fields, because software is changing everything.

Redi Hoffman

In this chapter, you will learn how to solve some of the most common string-based technical interview questions. While you most likely won't have to find anagrams at your software engineering job, learning how to detect them teaches you to solve problems using concepts such as sorting, which you will have to do. Furthermore, other things you will learn in this chapter, such as modular arithmetic and list comprehensions, will be useful in your day-to-day programming.

Anagram Detection

Two strings are **anagrams** if they contain the same letters, but not necessarily in the same order (case does not matter). For example, *Car* and *arc* are anagrams. The key to determining whether two strings are anagrams is to sort them. If the sorted strings are the same, they are anagrams. Here is how to write an algorithm that determines whether two strings are anagrams:

```
def is_anagram(s1, s2):
    s1 = s1.replace(' ','').lower()
    s2 = s2.replace(' ','').lower()
    if sorted(s1) == sorted(s2):
        return True
    else:
        return False

s1 = 'Emperor Octavian'
s2 = 'Captain over Rome'
print(is_anagram(s1,s2))

>> True
```

Anagrams sometimes contain multiple words and include uppercase and lowercase letters, so you start your function by removing spaces from your strings and converting all the characters to lowercase:

```
s1 = s1.replace(' ','').lower()
s2 = s2.replace(' ','').lower()
```

You then sort both strings and compare the result to determine whether they are the same. If they are, the strings are anagrams, and you return True. Otherwise, they are not, and you return False.

```
if sorted(s1) == sorted(s2):
    return True
else:
    return False
```

Because your algorithm to detect anagrams relies on Python's built-in sorted function, its run time is $O(n \log n)$.

Palindrome Detection

A **palindrome** is a word that reads the same backward as forward. *Hannah*, *mom*, *wow*, and *racecar* are all examples of palindromes. There are several ways to determine whether a string is a palindrome. One way is to copy the string, reverse it, and compare it to the original. If they are equal, the string is a palindrome.

Here is how to reverse a string in Python:

```
print("blackswan"[::-1])

>> nawskcalb
```

Here is how to check whether a string is a palindrome:

```
def is_palindrome(s1):
    if s1.lower() == s1[::-1].lower():
        return True
    return False
```

First, you use Python's built-in lower function to make sure capitalization doesn't affect your comparison. Then, you use Python's slicing syntax to reverse the string and compare it to the original:

```
if s1.lower() == s1[::-1].lower():
```

If the two strings are the same, the string is a palindrome, and you return True:

```
return True
```

Otherwise, the strings are not palindromes, and you return `False`:

```
Return False
```

The slowest part of your algorithm to detect palindromes is Python's syntax for reversing a list. Because Python has to visit every item in a list to reverse it, the run time to reverse a list is O(n), which makes your algorithm's run time O(n) as well.

Last Digit

Another common interview question is to return the rightmost digit in a string. For example, given the string `"Buy 1 get 2 free"`, your function should return the number 2.

One elegant way to solve this problem is to use Python's list comprehension feature. A list **comprehension** is Python syntax for creating a new, altered list from an existing iterable (like another list).

Here is the syntax for a list comprehension:

```
new_list = [expression(i) for i in iterable if filter(i)]
```

`iterable` is the iterable you are using to create your new list. `expression(i)` is a variable that holds each element from `iterable`. For example, in this regular expression, c contains each character in the string `"selftaught"`.

```
print([c for c in "selftaught"])
>> ['s', 'e', 'l', 'f', 't', 'a', 'u', 'g', 'h', 't']
```

As you can see, Python returns a list that contains all the letters from your original string `"selftaught"`.

`filter(i)` allows you to make changes to the original iterable. For example, you can create a filter that adds items to your iterable only if they meet your filter's requirements:

```
print([c for c in "selftaught" if ord(c) > 102])
>> ['s', 'l', 't', 'u', 'g', 'h', 't']
```

Python's built-in function `ord` returns the ASCII code for a letter. In this case, you added a filter that adds characters to your iterable only if the character's ASCII code is greater than 102 (the letter *f*). As you can see, your new list is missing the letters *e*, *f*, and *a*.

You can use Python's `isdigit` function to filter everything except numbers:

```
s = "Buy 1 get 2 free"
nl = [c for c in s if c.isdigit()]
print(nl)

>> ['1', '2']
```

Now that you know how to use a list comprehension to find all the digits in a string, there is only one more step to find the rightmost digit, namely, using a negative index to get the last digit from your new list:

```
s = "Buy 1 get 2 free"
nl =[c for c in s if c.isdigit()][-1]
print(nl)

>> 2
```

First, your list comprehension returns a list of all the digits in your string. Then, you use a negative index to get the last item in your new list of numbers, which is the rightmost digit in your original string.

As you can see, you can use a list comprehension to turn three or four lines of code into one elegant line, which will help you write short, readable code when you are programming professionally.

Because your algorithm iterates through every character in the string to check whether it is a digit and reverses a list, its run time is $O(n)$.

Caesar Cipher

A **cipher** is an algorithm for encryption or decryption. Julius Caesar, the famous Roman general and politician, protected his confidential messages by encrypting them using an ingenious cipher. First, he would pick a number. Then, he would shift every letter by that number. For example, if he chose the number 3, the string *abc* would become *def*.

If the shift took him past the alphabet's end, he rotated back to the front of the alphabet. For example, if he had to shift *z* two places, it would become *b*.

Modulo arithmetic is the key to coding a Caesar cipher. **Modulo arithmetic** is a type of arithmetic where numbers wrap around at a specific value. You should already be familiar with modulo arithmetic because you can tell time (Figure 5.1).

Figure 5.1: You use modulo arithmetic when you tell time.

For example, suppose there is a flight from New York to Lima, Peru, that leaves at 9 p.m. Suppose the two cities are in the same time zone, and the flight takes eight hours. What time will the flight arrive? Nine plus 8 is 17, but a 12-hour clock doesn't show 17. To determine the arrival time, you add 9 and 8 (17) and perform modulo 12 on the result.

```
17 % 12
```

Twelve divides into 17 one time, with a remainder of 5, which means the flight will arrive at 5 a.m. (Figure 5.2).

Figure 5.2: Eight hours after 9 is 5.

Modular arithmetic is helpful when you are writing any program involving time. For example, if you were building a website for processing flight times, you could use modular arithmetic to figure out what time a flight will land.

Now that you understand how modular arithmetic works, you can code a Caesar cipher by writing a function that takes a string and a number to shift each letter by and outputs a new, encrypted string:

```python
import string


def cipher(a_string, key):
    uppercase = string.ascii_uppercase
    lowercase = string.ascii_lowercase
    encrypt = ''
    for c in a_string:
        if c in uppercase:
            new = (uppercase.index(c) + key) % 26
            encrypt += uppercase[new]
        elif c in lowercase:
            new = (lowercase.index(c) + key) % 26
            encrypt += lowercase[new]
        else:
            encrypt += c
    return encrypt
```

Your function, `cipher`, accepts two parameters: `a_string`, which is the string you want to encrypt, and `key`, the number of places you are shifting each letter.

You start by using Python's built-in `string` module to create two strings that contain every character in the alphabet in both uppercase and lowercase:

```
import string


def cipher(a_string, key):
    uppercase = string.ascii_uppercase
    lowercase = string.ascii_lowercase
```

If you print uppercase and lowercase, the output looks like this:

```
>> 'abcdefghijklmnopqrstuvwxyz'
>> 'ABCDEFGHIJKLMNOPQRSTUVWXYZ'
```

Next, you create the variable `encrypt`, which starts as an empty string but later will hold your encrypted string:

```
encrypt = ''
```

Then, you iterate through your string, keeping track of each character in the variable `c`:

```
for c in a_string:
```

If the character is uppercase, you find the character's index in `uppercase` (which, remember, is `ABCDEFGHIJKLMNOPQRSTUVWXYZ`). Then you add `key` to that index, which will give you the new, encrypted character. For example, if the character is *A* and `key` is 2, first, you get the index of *A* in `uppercase`, which is index 0, and then add 2. Index 2 in `uppercase` is the letter *C*.

There is a problem with using this method to get the new character, though. What happens if you shift the letter *Z* one or more places? The letter *Z* is at index 25. If you add 2 to 25, you get index 27, which does not exist. Because *Z* is the last letter in the alphabet, you need to go to the alphabet's beginning to get the new, encrypted character. In this case, you need to get index 2, which is *C* (index 0 + 2).

You solve this by using modulo 26 on the sum of each character's starting index plus `key`. First, you get the character's starting index in `uppercase`. Then, you add `key` and perform modulo 26.

```
if c in uppercase:
    new = (uppercase.index(c) + key) % 26
```

This code works because you are using modular arithmetic to "wrap around" whenever you reach a certain value. In this situation, you "wrap around" whenever your index exceeds 25.

Once you have the new index for the encrypted character, you use it to look up what character it is in `uppercase` and store it in the variable `encrypt`.

```
encrypt += uppercase[new]
```

If the character is lowercase, you do the same thing but use lowercase instead:

```
elif c in lowercase:
    new = (lowercase.index(c) + key) % 26
    encrypt += lowercase[new]
```

If the character isn't in uppercase or lowercase, it is a special character, so you add it to encrypt without making any changes:

```
else:
    encrypt += c
```

At the end of your loop, you return your new, encrypted string:

```
return encrypt
```

Because your algorithm only has to iterate through every letter in the string to encrypt it, its run time is O(n).

Vocabulary

anagrams: Two strings that contain the same letters, but not necessarily in the same order (case does not matter).

palindrome: A word that reads the same backward as forward.

list comprehension: Python syntax to create a new, altered list from an existing iterable (like another list).

cipher: An algorithm for encryption or decryption.

modulo arithmetic: A type of arithmetic where numbers wrap around at a specific value.

Challenge

1. Use a list comprehension to return a list of all the words in the following list that have more than four characters: ["selftaught", "code", "sit", "eat", "programming", "dinner", "one", "two", "coding", "a", "tech"].

6 Math

> *Do not worry too much about your difficulties in mathematics, I can assure you that mine are still greater.*
>
> Albert Einstein

In this chapter, you will learn some basic math that will help you pass a technical interview and improve as a programmer. While searching for prime numbers might not help you in your day-to-day programming, understanding the different algorithms you can use to find them will make you a better programmer. And while testing your ability to use the modulo operator in your algorithms is one of the most common technical interview "gotchas," the modulo operator can also be handy in real-world applications. Finally, this chapter introduces the concept of boundary conditions. If you create applications without thinking about boundary conditions, you will likely produce a website or app filled with unexpected errors, so it is important to learn what they are and how to prepare for them.

Binary

Computers "think" in binary. A **binary number** is a number in the base 2 numeral system. A **numeral system** is a writing system for expressing numbers. In base 2, numbers have only two digits: 0 and 1. In binary, a digit is called a **bit**, which stands for binary digit. The number system you are used to counting in is called base 10, and it has 10 digits (zero through nine). A numeral system's **base** is the number of digits the system has. The binary and decimal numeral systems are not the only number systems. There are also other numeral systems like base 16, called the *hexadecimal system*, which is popular with programmers.

Here are some examples of binary numbers:

```
100
1000
101
1101
```

When you are looking at these numbers, you do not know if they are in base 2 or base 10. For example, the first number, 100, could be either 100 in base 10 or 4 in base 2.

There are several notations you can use to show a number is base 2. For example, computer scientists often put a b before a number to show the number is in base 2. Here are other ways to indicate that a number is in base 2:

```
100b
1000₂
%100
0b100
```

A **place value** is the numerical value a digit has because of its position in a number. For example, a four-digit number has place values that represent thousands, hundreds, tens, and ones. For example, the number 1,452 is one thousand, plus four hundreds, plus five tens, plus two ones (Figure 6.1).

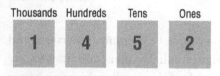

Figure 6.1: The place values for the number 1,452 in base 10

In the decimal system, each place value is a power of 10. The rightmost place value is 10 to the zero power, which is 1. The next place value is 10 to the first power, which is 10. The next place value is 10 to the second power (10 × 10), which is 100. The next place value is 10 to the third power (10 × 10 × 10), which is 1000 (Figure 6.2).

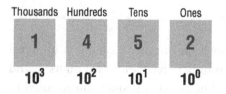

Figure 6.2: The powers of 10 used in the place values in base 10

You can express the number 1,452 as an equation using its place values:

```
(1 * 10 ** 3) + (4 * 10 ** 2) + (5 * 10 ** 1) + (2 * 10 ** 0) = 1452
```

Or visualize it as follows:

```
1 * 10 ** 3 = 1 * 1000 = 1000 +
4 * 10 ** 2 = 4 * 100 = 400 +
5 * 10 ** 1 = 5 * 10 = 50 +
```

```
2 * 10 ** 0 = 2 * 1 = 2
                        ─────────
                        1452
```

The binary number system works the same way as the decimal system, except there are only two digits, 0 and 1, and the place values are powers of 2, instead of powers of 10.

The rightmost place value is 2 to the zero power, which is 1. The next place value is 2 to the first power, which is 2. The next place value is 2 to the second power, which is 4 (2×2). The next place value is 2 to the third power, which is 8 ($2 \times 2 \times 2$) (Figure 6.3).

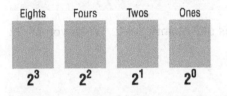

Figure 6.3: The powers of 2 used in the place values in base 2

Here is an equation that represents the number 1101 in base 2:

```
(1 * 2 ** 3) + (1 * 2 ** 2) + (0 * 2 ** 1)
+ (1 * 2 ** 0) =

8 + 4 + 0 + 1 = 13
```

Or:

```
1 * 2 ** 3 = 1 * 8 = 8 +
1 * 2 ** 2 = 1 * 4 = 4 +
0 * 2 ** 1 = 0 * 2 = 0 +
1 * 2 ** 0 = 1 * 1 = 1

                ─────
                  13
```

As you can see, 1101 in binary is 13 in base 10.

In the decimal system, you count by starting at zero: 0, 1, 2, 3, 4, 5, 6, 7, 8, 9. At that point, you run out of digits. To represent the next number, as you know, you create 10 by using 2 digits. You represent 10 with a 1 followed by a 0.

When you count in binary, you also start with zero.

```
0
```

And like the decimal system, the next number is 1.

```
1
```

After 1, you run out of digits. That means you need to use two digits to represent the number 2, just like you have to use two digits in the decimal system to represent the number 10.

In binary, you represent 2 with a 1 and a 0:

```
10
```

The 0 stands for no 1s, and the 1 stands for one quantity of 2.

How do you represent the number 3 in binary?

```
11
```

The first 1 means one quantity of 1, and the second 1 means one quantity of 2. When you add 2 and 1, you get 3.

Next up is 4, which in binary is as follows:

```
100
```

The first 0 means no ones, the second 0 means no twos, and the 1 means one quantity of four. Add them up, and you get 4.

Bitwise Operators

Usually, when you are programming and dealing with numbers, you work with integers and floats like 100 and 10.5. There are times, however, when it is useful for you to work with binary numbers instead. For example, working with binary numbers can help you quickly solve problems such as determining whether a number is a power of 2.

You can use the `bin` method to work with binary numbers in Python.

```
print(bin(16))

>> 0b1000
```

When you print `bin(16)`, the result is `0b10000`, which is 16 in binary. As you learned earlier, `0b` lets you know the number is in binary.

A **bitwise operator** is an operator you can use in an expression with two binary numbers. For example, Python's bitwise AND operator performs Boolean arithmetic bit by bit. When both bits are 1 (`True`), Python returns 1; otherwise, Python returns 0 (`False`). The logic for each bit in bitwise AND is the same as the keyword `and` in Python. As you know, when you use Python's keyword `and`, if both sides of the expression are `True`, Python returns `True`.

```
print(1==1 and 2==2)
>> True
```

If both sides are False, it returns False.

```
print(1==2 and 2==3)
>> False
```

If one side is True and the other is False, it returns False as well.

```
print(1==1 and 1==2)
>> False
```

Let's look at an example of using bitwise AND. Say you have two integers, 2 and 3. Two in binary is 0b10, and 3 is 0b11. The first bit of 2 is 0, and the first bit of 3 is 1.

```
10 # 2
11 # 3
──
 0
```

Applying bitwise AND to these bits produces 0 because there is a True and a False, which returns False (remember: 0 is False and 1 is True). Applying bitwise AND to the second set of bits produces 1 because both binary digits are True, so Python returns True.

```
10 # 2
11 # 3
──
10
```

In this case, the bitwise AND operation produces 0b10, which is the number 2 in binary (you will learn why this is useful shortly).

In Python, the bitwise AND operator is the ampersand symbol (&). Here is how you can use bitwise AND on the binary numbers 0b10 and 0b11 in Python:

```
print(0b10 & 0b11)

>> 2
```

You don't have to use a bitwise operator like bitwise AND on binary numbers.

```
print(2 & 3)

>> 2
```

In this case, you evaluated bitwise AND on decimal numbers, but Python uses the binary values for 2 and 3 to carry out the operation.

Python also has a bitwise OR operator, which operates bit by bit and returns 1 when one or more of the two bits is True and returns False when both are False, just like the or keyword in Python. For example, let's take a look at what happens when you use the bitwise OR operator on the numbers 2 and 3. Applying bitwise OR to the first two bits produces 1 because one of the bits is True.

```
10 # 2
11 # 3
—
 1
```

When you use bitwise OR on the second set of bits, Python returns 1 because both bits are True (1).

```
10 # 2
11 # 3
—
11
```

As you can see, the result of bitwise OR on 2 and 3 is 0b11, which is the decimal number 3. In Python, the bitwise OR operator is the pipe symbol (|).

```
print(2 | 3)
>> 3
```

The binary operators you've learned about so far are some of the most common; however, there are other binary operators like bitwise XOR, bitwise NOT, bitwise right shift, and bitwise left shift you can learn about in Python's documentation.

Let's take a look at some situations where bitwise operators are helpful. You can use the bitwise AND operator to check whether a number is even or odd. An even number like 2 always has a 0 at the end, whereas the number 1 always has a 1 at the end (and contains only one binary digit: 1).

```
10 # 2
 1 # 1
```

When you use bitwise AND on an even number and 1, Python will always return False because the even number will end with a 0, and 1 has only one binary digit: 1.

```
10 # 2
 1 # 1
--
 0
```

On the other hand, when you use bitwise AND on an odd number and 1, Python will always return True because the odd number will end with a 1, and 1 has only one binary digit: 1.

```
11 #3
 1 #1
--
 1
```

Because 1 has only one digit in binary, it doesn't matter if the number you are checking for evenness has one binary digit or one thousand. Because 1 has only one binary digit, you make only one comparison: the last binary digit in the number and 1.

Here is how to check if a number is even or odd using the AND bitwise operator in Python:

```
def is_even(n):
    return not n & 1
```

In your function is_even, you return not n & 1. Your code n & 1 uses the bitwise AND operator on n and 1. Then, you use not to change the result to the opposite of whatever it would have been, because when you perform bitwise AND on an even number and 1, it returns False, which means the number is even. In this case, you want your function to return True to represent that the number is even, so you use not to switch True to False and False to True.

You can also use the bitwise AND operator to see if an integer is a power of 2. Every number that is a power of 2 has a single 1 in its binary representation because binary is base 2, which means any power of 2 has only a single 1. For example, the number 8 is 0b1000 in binary. Conversely, a number that is 1 less than a power of 2 contains all 1 bits. For example, the number 7, which is 1 less than 8, is 0b111 in binary.

When you apply the bitwise AND operator to these two binary numbers, you can see the resulting binary will be all zeros when the first number is a power of 2.

```
1000 # 8
0111 # 7
-----
0000
```

If the number is not a power of 2, there will be at least one binary digit that is a 1.

```
0111 # 7
0110 # 6
-----
0001
```

Here is how to use the bitwise AND operator in Python to determine if a number is a power of 2:

```
def is_power(n):
    if n & (n - 1) == 0:
        return True
    return False
```

Your function `is_power` takes the number in question. Inside your function, you use an `if` statement to check if using bitwise AND on n and n − 1 is equal to 0. If it is, n is a power of 2, and you return `True`. Otherwise, it is not, and you return `False`.

FizzBuzz

FizzBuzz is one of the all-time classic interview challenges. I once heard a story about an engineer interviewing for a principal software engineer position, and they asked him to solve FizzBuzz. He couldn't, and he was very embarrassed. Don't worry, though; you are about to learn how to solve it, so that won't happen to you.

Here's the FizzBuzz challenge: write a program that prints the numbers from 1 to 100. If the number is a multiple of 3, print "Fizz." If the number is a multiple of 5, print "Buzz." If the number is a multiple of 3 and 5, print "FizzBuzz."

The key to this challenge is using the modulo operator, which divides two values and returns the remainder. If the remainder is 0, you know the dividend (the number you divided) is a multiple of the divisor (the number you divided by). For example, 6 % 3 divides 6 by 3 and returns a remainder of 0.

```
print(6 % 3)

>> 0
```

Because there is no remainder, you know 6 is a multiple of 3.

When you evaluate 7 % 3, there is a remainder, so you know 7 is not a multiple of 3.

```
print(7 % 3)
>> 1
```

To solve FizzBuzz, you iterate through the numbers 1 to 100 and use modulo to check whether each number is a multiple of 3 and 5, only 3, or only 5.

Here is how you do it:

```
def fizzbuzz(n):
    for i in range(1, n + 1):
        if i % 3 == 0 and i % 5 == 0:
            print('FizzBuzz')
        elif i % 3 == 0:
            print('Fizz')
        elif i % 5 == 0:
            print('Buzz')
        else:
            print(i)
```

Even though you want to find the numbers from 1 to 100, it is best to pass in a number, n, instead of hard-coding 100. Passing in n makes your program flexible if you want to run your program with a different number. So, your function, fizzbuzz, accepts n as a parameter.

```
def fizzbuzz(n):
```

First, you use a for loop to iterate through each number from 1 to n + 1.

```
for i in range(1, n + 1):
```

Then, you use a conditional statement with the modulo operator to determine if the number, i, is divisible by both 3 and 5. If it is, you print "FizzBuzz."

```
if i % 3 == 0 and i % 5 == 0:
    print('FizzBuzz')
```

Next, you use another conditional statement to check if the number is divisible by 3. If it is, you print "Fizz."

```
elif i % 3 == 0:
    print('Fizz')
```

Then you use one more conditional statement to see if the number is divisible by 5. If it is, you print "Buzz."

```
elif i % 5 == 0:
    print('Buzz')
```

If the number is not divisible by 3, 5, or both, you print the number.

```
else:
    print(i)
```

When you run your program, you will see that numbers that are divisible by 3, like 6 and 27, say "Fizz." Numbers that are divisible by 5, like 10 and 85, say "Buzz," and numbers divisible by both, like 15 and 30, say "FizzBuzz."

```
>> 1 2 Fizz 4 Buzz Fizz 7 8...Buzz Fizz 97 98 Fizz Buzz
```

Your algorithm takes n steps, which means it is linear. If you pass in 100, your algorithm will take 100 steps, and if you pass in 1000, it will take 1,000 steps.

The modulo operator was the key to solving this problem. The modulo operator is not just useful in technical interviews, though. It is also useful when you are building real-world applications. For example, say you have a text file that is 50,000 lines long, and you can fit 49 lines on a page.

How much text will there be on the last page? The last page will have 20 lines because 50,000 % 49 = 20. What if you had a database with 20,000 items in it and you wanted to do something to every other item? One way to accomplish this is to iterate through each item and only change items with an even index.

Greatest Common Factor

The **greatest common factor** is the largest positive integer that evenly divides two or more other integers. In this chapter, you will learn, given two integers, such as 20 and 12, how to find their greatest common factor.

In the case of 20 and 12, you can evenly divide them both by 1, 2, and 4. Since 4 is the largest number, it is their greatest common factor.

Factors of 20: 1, 2, 4, 5, 10

Factors of 12: 1, 2, 3, 4, 6

One algorithm for finding the greatest common factor of two numbers is to check all possible divisors to see which ones divide evenly into both numbers. For example, to find the greatest common factor of 20 and 12, you can start by dividing them both by 1, then 1, then 3, etc. You do not need to test any numbers greater than the smaller of the two numbers because a number larger than the smallest number could not divide evenly into it. For example, a number greater than 12 does not divide evenly into 12.

Here is the Python code for your algorithm:

```
def gcf(i1, i2):
    gcf = None
    if i1 > i2:
        smaller = i2
    else:
        smaller = i1
    for i in range(1, smaller + 1):
        if i1 % i == 0 and i2 % i == 0:
            gcf = i
    return gcf

gcf(20, 12)
```

Your function `gfc` accepts as parameters the two positive integers of which you are looking for the greatest common factor.

```
def gcf(i1, i2):
```

Inside your function, you determine which of the two integers is smaller and assign it to the variable `smaller` so that you can stop testing divisors once you hit that number.

```
if i1 > i2:
    smaller = i2
else:
    smaller = i1
```

Next, you use a `for` loop to test each divisor from 1 to the value of the variable `smaller` plus 1 (so that you also test the smaller number).

```
for i in range(1, smaller + 1):
```

Next, you use an `if` statement to see if the divisor divides evenly into both integers. If it does, you assign the divisor to the variable `gcf`.

```
if i1 % i == 0 and i2 % i == 0:
    gcf = div
```

Just because you found one common factor doesn't mean you've found the greatest common factor, however. If you find another, larger divisor, you set `gcf` to it the next time around your loop. That way, when your loop ends, `gfc` will contain the largest divisor.

There is a problem with your code, though. What if one of the integers is 0?

```
print(gcf(0, 22))

>> None
```

Your program returns the wrong answer when one of the integers is 0.

Your code's inability to handle 0 is an example of a **boundary condition**: input outside of the input you expected your program to receive. When calculating the greatest common factor of two numbers, if either of the integers is 0, the greatest common factor is the other integer. For example, the greatest common factor of 0 and 12 is 12.

When you are writing algorithms, you should always think about what sort of unexpected input could break it. In this case, your algorithm is incorrect when the input is 0. Here is how to modify your program to return the correct output if either of the integers is 0:

```
def gcf(i1, i2):
    if i1 == 0:
        return i2
    if i1 == 0:
        return i1

    if i1 > i2:
        smaller = i2
    else:
```

```
        smaller = i1

    for divisor in range(1, smaller + 1):
        if(i1 % divisor == 0) and (i2 % divisor == 0):
            gcf = divisor

    return gcf
```

Your program also cannot handle negative numbers, so you should add a test at the beginning to ensure both numbers are positive.

```
def gcf(i1, i2):
    if i1 < 0 or i2 < 0:
        raise ValueError("Numbers must be positive.")
    if i1 == 0:
        return i2
    if i1 == 0:
        return i

    if i1 > i2:
        smaller = i2
    else:
        smaller = i1

    for divisor in range(1, smaller+1):
        if(i1 % divisor == 0) and (i2 % divisor == 0):
            gcf = divisor

    return gcf
```

Your greatest common factor code is linear because your algorithm solves the problem in n steps. Linear is not bad, but there is a better way to solve this problem.

Euclid's Algorithm

A more efficient solution for finding the greatest common factor is called Euclid's algorithm. First, you divide one number, x, by the other number, y, to find the remainder. Then, you divide again, using the remainder for y and the previous y as the new x. You continue this process until the remainder is 0. The last divisor is the greatest common factor.

For example, to find the greatest common factor of 20 and 12, you start by dividing 20 by 12 (or 12 by 20) and get the remainder: 8. Next, you divide 12 by the remainder, and 12 divided by 8 produces a remainder of 4. Now, you divide 8 by 4. This time, there is no remainder, which means 4 is the greatest common factor.

20 / 12 = 1 remainder 8

12 / 8 = 1 remainder 4

8 /4 = 2 remainder 0

Here is Euclid's algorithm in Python:

```
def gcf(x, y):
    if y == 0:
        x, y = y, x
    while y != 0:
        x, y = y, x % y
    return x
```

Your `gcf` function accepts as parameters the two numbers of which you are looking for the greatest common factor.

In the first line of code, you address a boundary condition. If y is 0, Python will raise an exception later in your program, trying to divide by 0. If y is 0, you swap the contents of the variables x and y to solve this problem.

```
if y == 0:
    x, y = y, x
```

Next, you create a `while` loop that iterates until y becomes 0.

```
while y != 0:
```

Inside your `while` loop, this statement swaps the values in x and y with y and the remainder of x divided by y.

```
x, y = y, x % y
```

When your `while` loop ends, it means x % y returned a remainder of 0. You then return the value of x, which holds the greatest common factor of x and y.

```
return x
```

You can use math to prove this algorithm is logarithmic rather than linear, significantly improving its performance with large numbers over your original algorithm in finding the greatest common factor of two numbers.

Primes

A **prime number** is a positive integer divisible only by itself and 1. Numbers like 2, 3, 5, 7, and 11 are examples of prime numbers. In this section, you will learn how to write a function that determines if a number is a prime or not.

Here is how you do it:

```
def is_prime(n):
    for i in range(2, n):
        if n % i == 0:
            return False
    return True
```

Your function is_prime, takes the number you want to check whether or not it is a prime (n).

```
def is_prime(n):
```

You then use a for loop to iterate through every number from 2 to n. You start with 2 (not 1) because prime numbers are still divisible by 1.

```
for i in range(2, n):
```

If n is 10, your code will iterate from 2 to 9, which means 10 gets skipped (you want this to happen because prime numbers are also divisible by themselves).

Next, you use modulo to check whether there is a remainder when you divide n by i. If there is no remainder, you found a divisor other than 1 or the number. That means n is not a prime number, so you return False.

```
if n % i == 0:
    return False
```

If you've iterated through your number range without finding a divisor, it means n is a prime, and you return True.

```
return True
```

Because your algorithm takes n steps to complete, it is a linear algorithm.

You can improve your algorithm by ending your loop at the square root of n instead of at n − 1.

```
import math

def is_prime(n):
    for i in range(2, int(math.sqrt(n)) + 1):
        if n % i == 0:
            return False
    return True
```

Here is why you can stop at the square root of n. If a * b == n, then either a or b has to be less than or equal to the square root of n. Why? Because if both a and b are greater than the square root of n, then a * b has to be greater than n and, therefore, cannot equal n. So, you cannot have two numbers, a and b, where both are larger than the square root of n, multiply to become n since a * b will be greater than n. Since one divisor must be less than or equal to the square root of n, you don't have to test up to n. Instead, you can stop at the first integer larger than the square root of n. If you don't find any number less than or equal to the square root of n that divides n evenly, then you won't find any number that does.

You can easily modify your program to print a list of all the prime numbers within a number range.

```
def is_prime(n):
    for i in range(2, int(math.sqrt(n)) + 1):
        if n % i == 0:
            return False
    return True


def find_primes(n):
    return [i for i in range(2, n) if is_prime(i)]
```

First, you create a new function called find_primes, which takes as a parameter n, which is the number up to which you are looking for primes.

You then use a list comprehension to iterate from 2 to n, only adding items to your new list if is_prime returns True.

```
return [is_prime(i) for i in range(2, n)]
```

Your algorithm to find all the prime numbers in a number range calls your linear is_prime function inside a loop, which means it has an O(n**2) time complexity and is not very efficient. The algorithm you learned in this chapter is not the only algorithm for finding prime numbers, though. There are other, more complicated algorithms to find prime numbers that have a more efficient time complexity you can learn as well.

Vocabulary

greatest common factor: The largest positive integer that evenly divides two or more other integers.

boundary condition: Input outside of the standard input you expect your program to receive.

prime number: A positive integer divisible only by itself and 1.

bitwise operator: An operator you can use in an expression with two binary numbers.

binary number: A number in the base 2 numeral system.

numeral system: A writing system for expressing numbers.

bit: In binary, a digit is called a bit, which stands for binary digit.

base: A numeral system's base is the number of digits the system has.

place value: The numerical value a digit has because of its position in a number.

Challenge

1. Research and write another way to find prime numbers.

7 Self-Taught Inspiration: Margaret Hamilton

All of my friends who have younger siblings who are going to college or high school—my number-one piece of advice is: you should learn how to program.

Mark Zuckerberg

Today, there are so many resources to teach yourself how to program; it is easy to forget it wasn't always that way. Margaret Hamilton, one of the original coders on the Apollo space mission and one of the greatest self-taught programmers of all time, made her mark on technology long before programming courses were widely available.

While Hamilton did go to college (she received a B.A. from the University of Michigan in mathematics), her programming skills were entirely self-taught. In the 1950s and '60s, everyone was self-taught because computer science as we know it did not exist yet, so programmers had to figure things out on their own. At the time, the word *software engineering* didn't even exist: Hamilton helped coin it! After she graduated from college in 1960, Hamilton began her programming career working at MIT on software called Project Whirlwind to predict the weather. While she was at MIT, she helped create the code for the world's first portable computer.

Hamilton's success with Project Whirlwind led to a position with SAGE, an organization that helped detect potential Soviet airstrikes during the Cold War. If you're a *Star Trek* fan, you'll know the story of the Kobayashi Maru—a training exercise for Starfleet cadets that was unwinnable. Future officers might not have been able to beat the game, but they could show important character traits through their choices. Hamilton encountered a real-life Kobayashi Maru situation and, like the infamous Captain Kirk, managed to beat it. Every newcomer to SAGE was given a practically unsolvable program and tasked with getting it to run. The programmer who created it even wrote comments in Greek and Latin to make the challenge harder. Hamilton was the first engineer to get it to run, which secured her place within the organization.

Her ability to solve difficult problems got her hired for NASA's Apollo mission, culminating in Neil Armstrong, Buzz Aldrin, and Michael Collins landing on the moon in 1969. While the astronauts get the most credit for the historic mission, more than 400,000 people contributed to it, and Hamilton was instrumental to its success.

One of her team's most significant accomplishments was developing a system that could alert the team about emergencies. This process was a critical part of the moon landing's success and benefited greatly from Hamilton's insistence on rigorous testing. Dr. Paul Curto, who nominated her for a NASA Space Act Award, said her work comprised the "foundation for ultra-reliable software design" because, to date, no one has found a bug in the Apollo software.

On November 22, 2016, President Barack Obama awarded Hamilton the Presidential Medal of Freedom to recognize her outstanding software engineering achievements and cementing her position as one of the greatest self-taught programmers of all time.

Data Structures

8   What Is a Data Structure?

Algorithms + Data Structures = Programs.

Niklaus Wirth

A **data structure** is a way of organizing data in a computer so programmers can effectively use it in their programs. Throughout this book, you've already used some of Python's built-in data structures such as lists and dictionaries to search data, sort data, and more. This section of the book will teach you more about data structures and how to use them. You will also learn about new types of data structures you may not be familiar with yet, such as arrays, linked lists, stacks, queues, trees, heaps, graphs, and hash tables. Each of these data structures has advantages and disadvantages. The best data structure to use in a program depends on what type of problem you are trying to solve and what you are trying to optimize for. In Part II of this book, you will learn about the pros and cons of different data structures so that when you are building applications, you can decide what the best data structure to use will be. Plus, you will learn how to answer the most common questions interviewers ask about data structures so that when it comes time for you to go through a technical interview, you will pass with flying colors.

You cannot be a great programmer without a solid understanding of data structures because programming means writing algorithms and choosing the right data structure to go with them. That is why Niklaus Wirth famously wrote, "Algorithms + Data Structures = Programs." The algorithm tells your computer what to do, and your data structure tells your computer how to store the data from your algorithm. Linux Torvalds, the creator of Linux, stressed the importance of data structures even more with his famous quote, "I will, in fact, claim that the difference between a bad programmer and a good one is whether he considers his code or his data structures more important. Bad programmers worry about the code. Good programmers worry about data structures and their relationships." I want you to be a good programmer, which is why I will focus on teaching you about data structures for the remainder of this book.

An **abstract data type** is a description of a data structure, whereas a data structure is an actual implementation. For example, a list is an abstract data type: it describes a data structure that holds a group of items where each item has a position relative to the others. A list also has operations to manipulate its items, like adding and removing them. When you use a Python list, you are using a data structure, not an abstract data type, because a data structure is the actual implementation of an abstract data type. For example, Python could have two different list data structures, implemented in entirely different ways, both based on the list abstract data type.

Computer scientists classify data structures based on different properties, for example, whether they are linear or nonlinear. A **linear data structure** arranges data elements in a sequence, while a **nonlinear data structure** links data nonsequentially. For example, Python lists are a linear data structure: each element can have one element before and one element after it. In contrast, graphs (which you will also learn more about later) are nonlinear structures where each element can connect to many other elements.

Traversing a data structure means going from the first element in a data structure to the last. In a linear data structure, you can easily traverse from the first element to the last without backtracking (moving backward in the data structure), whereas in a nonlinear data structure you often have to backtrack. It is often more efficient to access individual elements in a linear data structure because nonlinear data structures often require backtracking or recursion to access a single element. Because you can easily traverse a linear data structure, making a change to every element in one is often simpler than making a change to every element in a nonlinear structure. Because you don't have to backtrack to visit every element, linear data structures are often easier to design and use. Regardless, nonlinear data structures can be better (and more efficient) for certain kinds of problems. For example, you can use nonlinear data structures to store and access data that would be inefficient to store in a linear structure, such as the connections in a social network.

Computer scientists also classify data structures by whether they are static or dynamic. A **static data structure** has a fixed size, while a **dynamic data structure** can grow or shrink in size. Usually, you define the size of a static data structure when you create it in your program. Once you make it, your data structure's size is fixed and cannot change, but you can change the data's values inside it. Python does not have static data structures; however, lower-level programming languages like C do.

One problem with static data structures is that you must allocate a certain amount of memory for them. **Computer memory** is where your computer stores data. There are different kinds of memory, and explaining them all is outside the scope of this book, but for this chapter, you can think of memory as a place your computer stores data with an address it can use to reference it later. If the number of data elements you are working with ends up being smaller than the size you allocated, you've wasted memory space. Additionally, it may not be possible to add more elements than fit in the space you gave your data structure. Often the only way to add more elements to a static data structure is to allocate memory for a new structure big enough to contain the old and the new elements and then to copy the data from the old structure to this newly allocated memory together with the new elements. Because of this, static data structures are not the best data structure to use if you don't know the number of elements you need to store in advance. However, if you know how many data elements you want to store and that number is not likely to change, then a static data structure often outperforms a dynamic one. For example, if you are maintaining a list of "undo" functions for a program that allows users up to 10 undo operations, a static data structure would be appropriate.

Many data structures can be static or dynamic. For example, arrays (which we will discuss in the next chapter) are often static data structures, but many modern programming languages, such as Python, offer dynamic arrays (lists).

In contrast to static data structures, you can easily change the size of a dynamic data structure. In a dynamic data structure, your computer allocates additional memory as you add more elements. When you remove elements, your computer frees that memory for other data. With their flexible size, dynamic data structures allow you to add and remove data elements efficiently, and these structures make efficient use of memory resources. However, accessing elements in dynamic data structures can be slow compared to static data structures, and storing a certain number of elements in dynamic data structures can often consume more memory than storing the same number of elements in static data structures. When dealing with an unknown amount of data, especially in situations where memory space is limited, dynamic data structures are often a good choice.

Unless you are writing low-level code for an operating system or some other project where you have to squeeze out every possible performance optimization, you most likely will not spend a lot of time thinking about choosing a static or dynamic data structure. Instead, you will probably spend more time deciding whether you should use a linear or nonlinear data structure and, once you've made that decision, which linear or nonlinear data structure to use. As you learned earlier, different data structures have pros and cons. These pros and cons are mostly related to their efficiency in inserting, deleting, searching, and sorting data and how efficiently they use memory space. For example, it is incredibly efficient to check if an item is in a Python dictionary, even if it has a billion data pieces. It is not nearly as efficient to search a graph for a piece of data, though. In the next chapter, we'll dive into more detail about when and how to use data structures.

Vocabulary

data structure: A way of organizing data in a computer so programmers can effectively use it in their programs.

linear data structure: A data structure that arranges data elements in a sequence.

nonlinear data structure: A data structure that links data nonsequentially.

traversing: Going from the first element in a data structure to the last.

static data structure: A data structure with a fixed size.

dynamic data structure: A data structure that can grow or shrink in size.

computer memory: Where your computer stores data.

Challenge

1. Write a list of all the data structures you've used in Python.

9 Arrays

We salute the coders, designers, and programmers already hard at work at their desks, and we encourage every student who can't decide whether to take that computer science class to give it a try.
Michael Bloomberg, former mayor, New York City

A **list** is an abstract data type that describes a data structure that stores ordered values. Lists usually have an operation for creating a new, empty list, testing if it is empty, prepending an item, appending an item, and accessing an element at an index. You are already familiar with Python lists, one of many different implementations of the list abstract data type, which is a type of array. In this chapter, you will learn more about arrays.

An **array** is a data structure that stores elements with indexes in a contiguous block of memory. Arrays are often homogeneous and static. A **homogeneous data structure** can hold only a single data type, such as integers or strings. A static data structure is a data structure you cannot resize after you create it. When you create an array in a low-level programming language like C, you decide how many elements of a particular data type you want to store in it. Then, your computer assigns a block of memory for your array based on the number of elements and how much memory one element of that data type requires. This block consists of items stored one after the other in your computer's memory.

A Python list is a **heterogeneous variable-length array**. A **variable-length array** is one with a size that can change after you create it. A **heterogeneous array** is one that can hold different types of data rather than just a single type. Guido van Rossum wrote Python in C, but Python hides the complexities of array creation and manipulation. Instead, it presents you with a list data structure you can use without worrying about assigning its length ahead of time or specifying what data types it can hold.

Figure 9.1 shows an example of how a computer stores an array in its memory.

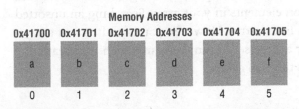

Figure 9.1: An example of data in an array

You can access each element in this array with a unique integer index. Usually, the first index in an array is index 0; however, different programming languages use different indexing schemes. Both Python and C use zero-based indexing, but some other languages, like MATLAB and Fortran, use one-based indexing (the first element is index 1). Some programming languages even allow you to use any integer value for the index of the first element. The memory location of the first element in an array is called its **base address**. When your computer needs to add a new item to an array, it calculates the location in memory it should put it in using this formula:

```
base_address + index * size_of_data_type
```

It takes the base address and adds it to the index multiplied by how much memory space the data type in the array takes up. Your computer also uses this formula when it needs to find an item in an array.

Arrays can be one-dimensional or multidimensional. In a **one-dimensional array**, you access each element in the array with an integer index:

```
array = [1, 2, 3]
print(array[0])

>> 1
```

In a **multidimensional array**, you access each individual element with two indexes (an integer index for each dimension):

```
multi_array = [[1, 2, 3], [4, 5, 6], [7, 8, 9]]
print(array[1][2])

>> 6
```

Regardless of whether an array is one-dimensional or multidimensional, your computer stores its elements in a contiguous block of memory and uses a mathematical formula that maps the index to a memory location to access them.

Array Performance

You can access and modify any single element in an array in constant time. For example, suppose you look up the data at index 3 in an array. In that case, your computer has to get information from only one memory location, even if there are a million elements in your array. Searching an unsorted array is O(n) because you need to check every item in the array. However, you can often sort arrays, like when you have a list of names or addresses, or a large set of numbers, in which case searching the array can be O(log n). Figure 9.2 shows the run times of arrays.

Data Structure	Time Complexity							
	Average				Worst			
	Access	Search	Insertion	Deletion	Access	Search	Insertion	Deletion
Array	O(1)	O(n)	O(n)	O(n)	O(1)	O(n)	O(n)	O(n)
Stack	O(n)	O(n)	O(1)	O(1)	O(n)	O(n)	O(1)	O(1)
Queue	O(n)	O(n)	O(1)	O(1)	O(n)	O(n)	O(1)	O(1)
Linked List	O(n)	O(n)	O(1)	O(1)	O(n)	O(n)	O(1)	O(1)
Hash Table	N/A	O(1)	O(1)	O(1)	N/A	O(n)	O(n)	O(n)
Binary Search Tree	O(log n)	O(log n)	O(log n)	O(log n)	O(n)	O(n)	O(n)	O(n)

Figure 9.2: Array operation run times

If arrays are so efficient, you might wonder why you shouldn't use them in every situation. While accessing and modifying individual elements in an array is very fast, modifying the shape of an array in any way (adding or deleting items) is O(n). Because your computer stores the elements in an array in a single continuous block of memory, inserting an element into an array means you have to shift all the elements coming after the added element, which is not efficient. For example, suppose you have an array that looks like Figure 9.3.

Memory Locations

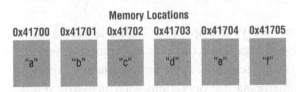

Figure 9.3: An array stored in a computer's memory

Look at what happens when you add z after a and b in Figure 9.4.

Memory Locations

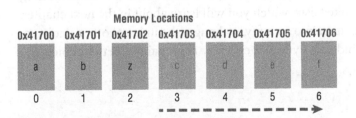

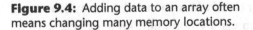

Figure 9.4: Adding data to an array often means changing many memory locations.

Making the third item in this list z requires your computer to shift four elements to different memory locations.

Having to shift elements is not a problem with small arrays, but if your program needs to add items to random locations in a large array (especially near the beginning), your computer may spend a lot of time copying memory around. This problem is worse for static arrays because your computer can't guarantee the memory addresses that come after the memory block it reserved for the array are free. That means when you add an element to an array in a language like C, you may need to reserve a new block of memory for the array, copy all the items from the old block to the new one, add the new element, and then free the old block. Python adds items to its lists more efficiently through a process called **overallocation**: reserving more memory for an array than it needs and keeping track of how many elements the array is storing and how much unused space it has.

As a programmer, you will frequently use arrays in your programs. You should consider using an array any time you need to store and access sequential data. For example, say you were programming a game like *Call of Duty* and you wanted to create a page that shows how the top 10 players rank. You could use an array to easily keep track of the top 10 players, their scores, and their order by storing the highest-ranking player at index 0 and the lowest ranking player at index 9. Arrays are one of the most important data structures for mathematical calculations. If you need to deal with large amounts of numerical data, you will get familiar with arrays. Computer scientists also use arrays to implement other data structures. For example, in later chapters you will learn how to implement stack and queue data structures using arrays.

Many programming languages' run-time systems use arrays to implement higher-level structures such as lists, which Python programmers use extensively. Arrays like the ones in Python's Numerical Python (NumPy) package are helpful for mathematical and scientific applications, financial applications, statistics, and so forth. NumPy arrays support mathematical operations such as matrix multiplication, which is used, for example, in graphics applications to scale, translate, and rotate graphical objects. In operating systems, arrays often handle any operation that manipulates a data sequence, such as memory management and buffering.

An array is not the best choice for large data sets you want to add data to often because adding items to an array is $O(n)$. In this situation, linked lists, which you will learn about in the next chapter, are often a better choice. When you insert an item into an array, it changes the index of other elements, so if you need your data to keep the same index, a Python dictionary is probably a better choice.

Creating an Array

If you are programming in Python, you can use a list in most cases when you need an array. However, if you need the performance of a homogenous array, you can use Python's built-in `array` class. Here is how it works:

```
import array

arr = array.array('f', (1.0, 1.5, 2.0, 2.5))
print(arr[1])

>> 1
```

First, you import Python's built-in `array` module:

```
import array
```

Then, you pass `array.array` two parameters. The first parameter tells Python what data type you want your array to hold. In this case, `f` stands for float (a data type in Python for decimal numbers), but you can also create an array with Python's other data types. The second parameter is a Python list containing the data you want to put into your array.

```
arr = array.array('f', (1.0, 1.5, 2.0, 2.5))
```

Once you've created your array, you can use it like a Python list:

```
print(arr[1])
```

However, if you try to add a piece of data to your array other than the data type you initially passed in, you will get an error:

```
arr[1] = 'hello'

>> TypeError: "must be real number, not str"
```

Python's NumPy package also offers an array you can use to make calculations run nearly as fast as a lower-level programming language like C. You can learn more about creating arrays with NumPy by reading its documentation at `numpy.org`.

Moving Zeros

In a technical interview, you might have to locate all the zeros in a list and push them to the end, leaving the remaining elements in their original order. For example, suppose you have this list:

```
[8, 0, 3, 0, 12]
```

You would take it and return a new list with all the zeros at the end, like this:

```
[8, 3, 12, 0, 0]
```

Here is how you solve this problem in Python:

```python
def move_zeros(a_list):
    zero_index = 0
    for index, n in enumerate(a_list):
        if n != 0:
            a_list[zero_index] = n
            if zero_index != index:
                a_list[index] = 0
            zero_index += 1
    return(a_list)

a_list = [8, 0, 3, 0, 12]
move_zeros(a_list)
print(a_list)
```

First, you create a variable called zero_index and set it to 0:

```python
zero_index = 0
```

Then, you loop through every number in a_list, using the enumerate function to keep track of both the index and the current number in the list:

```python
for index, n in enumerate(a_list):
```

Next comes this code, which executes only if n is not equal to 0:

```python
if n != 0:
    a_list[zero_index] = n
    if zero_index != index:
        a_list[index] = 0
    zero_index += 1
```

When n is not equal to 0, you use the index stored in zero_index to replace whatever is at zero_index with n. Then, you check to see if zero_index and index are no longer the same number. If they are not the same number, it means there was a zero earlier in the list, so you replace whatever number is at the current index with 0 and increment zero_index by 1.

Let's take a look at why this works. Say this is your list, and your algorithm just hit the first zero, which means index is 1.

```python
[8, 0, 3, 0, 12]
```

Because the number is a zero, this time around your loop, this code will not execute:

```python
if n != 0:
    a_list[zero_index] = n
```

```
    if zero_index != index:
        a_list[index] = 0
    zero_index += 1
```

That means you did not increment `zero_index`. The next time around your loop, `index` is 2, n is 3, and your list is still the same.

```
[8, 0, 3, 0, 12]
```

Because this time n is not 0, this code executes:

```
if n != 0:
    a_list[zero_index] = n
    if zero_index != index:
        a_list[index] = 0
    zero_index += 1
```

When this part of your code runs:

```
a_list[zero_index] = n
```

it changes your list from this:

```
[8, 0, 3, 0, 12]
```

to this:

```
[8, 3, 3, 0, 12]
```

Then, this line of code:

```
if zero_index != index:
    a_list[index] = 0
```

changes your list from this:

```
[8, 3, 3, 0, 12]
```

to this:

```
[8, 3, 0, 0, 12]
```

Your code swapped the zero in the back of the list to the next nonzero number toward the front of the list.

Now, your algorithm hits a zero again, and the same thing happens.

```
[8, 3, 0, 0, 12]
```

Your variable zero_index and index are no longer the same and zero_index is 3, which is the index of the 0 farthest back in the list. The next time around, n is 12, so this code executes again:

```
if n != 0:
    a_list[zero_index] = n
    if zero_index != index:
        a_list[index] = 0
    zero_index += 1
```

This code:

```
a_list[zero_index] = n
```

changes your list from this:

```
[8, 3, 0, 0, 12]
```

to this:

```
[8, 3, 12, 0, 12]
```

This code:

```
if zero_index != index:
    a_list[index] = 0
```

changes it from this:

```
[8, 3, 12, 0, 12]
```

to this:

```
[8, 3, 12, 0, 0]
```

As you can see, the zeros are now at the end of the list, with the rest of the numbers preceding them in their original order.

Your algorithm contains one main loop that iterates through the elements in a_list, which means its time complexity is O(n).

Combining Two Lists

When preparing for a technical interview, you should be prepared to combine two lists, something you will have to do often in your day-to-day programming. For example, suppose you have a list of movies:

```
movie_list = [ "Interstellar", "Inception",
```

```
                    "The Prestige", "Insomnia",
                    "Batman Begins"
          ]
```

and a list of ratings:

```
ratings_list = [1, 10, 10, 8, 6]
```

You want to combine these two sets of data into a single list of tuples containing each movie title and its rating, like this:

```
[('Interstellar', 1),
('Inception', 10),
('The Prestige', 10),
('Insomnia', 8),
('Batman Begins', 6)]
```

You can use Python's built-in `zip` function to combine these lists:

```
print(list(zip(movie_list, ratings_list)))

>> [('Interstellar', 1), ('Inception', 10), ('The Prestige', 10), ('Insomnia', 8),
('Batman Begins', 6)]
```

The `zip` function takes one or more iterables and returns a `zip` object containing one piece of data from each iterable, which you then turn into a list. Your output is a list of tuples, with each list containing the name of a movie matched to its rating.

Finding the Duplicates in a List

Another common technical interview question is to check for duplicate items in a list, which you will also have to do often in real-world programming. One solution is to compare each item in your list to every other item. Unfortunately, comparing every item to every other item requires two nested loops and is $O(n**2)$. Python sets provide a better way to look for duplicates. A **set** is a data structure that cannot contain duplicate elements. If a set has a string such as `'Kanye West'`, it is impossible to add another instance of `'Kanye West'` to it.

Here is how to create a set and add data to it:

```
a_set = set()
a_set.add("Kanye West")
a_set.add("Kendall Jenner")
a_set.add("Justin Bieber")
print(a_set)

>> {'Kanye West', 'Kendall Jenner', 'Justin Bieber'}
```

Your code creates a set with three strings in it: `"Kanye West"`, `"Kendall Jenner"`, and `"Justin Bieber"`. Now try to add a second instance of `"Kanye West"` to your set:

```
a_set = set()
a_set.add('Kanye West')
a_set.add('Kanye West')
a_set.add('Kendall Jenner')
a_set.add('Justin Bieber')
print(a_set)

>> {'Kanye West', 'Kendall Jenner', 'Justin Bieber'}
```

As you can see, your set still has only three items in it. Python did not add a second instance of `'Kanye West'` because it is a duplicate.

Since sets cannot contain duplicates, you can add items from an iterable to a set one by one, and if its length does not change, you know the item you are trying to add is a duplicate.

Here is a function that uses sets to check for the duplicates in a list:

```
def return_dups(an_iterable):
    dups = []
    a_set = set()

    for item in an_iterable:
        l1 = len(a_set)
        a_set.add(item)
        l2 = len(a_set)
        if l1 == l2:
            dups.append(item)
    return dups

a_list = [
    "Susan Adams",
    "Kwame Goodall",
    "Jill Hampton",
    "Susan Adams"]

dups = return_dups(a_list)
print(dups)
```

The list you are evaluating contains four elements with one duplicate: `"Susan Adams"`.

Your function `return_dups` accepts an iterable called `an_iterable` as a parameter:

```
def return_dups(an_iterable):
```

Inside your function, you create an empty list to hold the duplicates called `dups`:

```
dups = []
```

Then, you create an empty set called a_set:

```
a_set = set()
```

Next, you use a `for` loop to iterate through each item in `an_iterable`:

```
for item in an_iterable:
```

Next, you get the set's length, add an item from `an_iterable`, and check if the length changed:

```
l1 = len(a_set)
a_set.add(item)
l2 = len(a_set)
```

If your set's length did not change, the current item is a duplicate, so you append it to your `dups` list:

```
if l1 == l2:
    dups.append(item)
```

Here is your complete program:

```
def duplicates(an_iterable):
    dups = []
    a_set = set()
    for item in an_iterable:
        l1 = len(a_set)
        a_set.add(item)
        l2 = len(a_set)
        if l1 == l2:
            dups.append(item)
    return dups

a_list = [
    'Susan Adams',
    'Kwame Goodall',
    'Jill Hampton',
    'Susan Adams']

dups = duplicates(a_list)
print(dups)

>> ['Susan Adams']
```

When you run your function and pass in an iterable with duplicates, it outputs your `dups` list containing all the duplicates.

Finding the Intersection of Two Lists

Another common technical interview question involves writing a function to find the intersection of two lists, which is also helpful in your day-to-day programming. For example, say you have a list of winning lottery numbers in one list and another list that contains the most common winning lottery numbers of all time.

```
this_weeks_winners = [2, 43, 48, 62, 64, 28, 3]
most_common_winners = [1, 28, 42, 70, 2, 10, 62, 31, 4, 14]
```

Your goal is to find how many of the current winning numbers are in the winner's list.

One way to solve this problem is to use a list comprehension to create a third list and use a filter to check whether each value in list2 is also in list2:

```
def return_inter(list1, list2):
    list3 = [v for v in list1 if v in list2]
    return list3

list1 = [2, 43, 48, 62, 64, 28, 3]
list2 = [1, 28, 42, 70, 2, 10, 62, 31, 4, 14]
print(return_inter(list1, list2))

>> [2, 62, 28]
```

As you can see, the numbers 2, 62, and 28 are in both lists.

This line of code uses a `for` loop to walk through `list1` and appends the item to your new list only if that value is also in `list2`.

```
list3 = [v for v in list1 if v in list2]
```

Python's `in` keyword searches an iterable for a value. Because you are dealing with unordered lists, Python performs a linear search when you use the keyword `in` inside your list comprehension. Since you are using the `in` keyword inside a loop (the first part of the list comprehension), your algorithm's time complexity is $O(n**2)$.

Another option is to use a set to solve this problem. In Python, sets have an `intersection` function that returns any elements that appear in two or more sets.

You can easily change lists into sets like this:

```
set1 = set(list1)
set2 = set(list2)
```

Once you've converted your lists to sets, you can apply the intersection function to find out where the two sets have duplicate items. Here is the syntax for calling the `intersection` function on two sets:

```
set1.intersection(set2)
```

Next, you convert the intersected set back into a list using the `list` function:

```
list(set1.intersection(set2))
```

Let's put it all together:

```
def return_inter(list1, list2):
    set1 = set(list1)
    set2 = set(list2)
    return list(set1.intersection(set2))

list1 = [2, 43, 48, 62, 64, 28, 3]
list2 = [1, 28, 42, 70, 2, 10, 62, 31, 4, 14]
new_list = return_inter(list1, list2)
print(new_list)

>> [2, 28, 62]
```

The first line defines a function called `return_inter` that accepts two lists as parameters:

```
def return_inter(list1, list2):
```

Next, you convert the lists into sets:

```
set1 = set(list1)
set2 = set(list2)
```

Then you call the `intersection` function and find the duplicates:

```
list(set1.intersection(set2))
```

Finally, you convert the set back into a list and return the result:

```
return list(set1.intersection(set2))
```

You are not limited to using the `intersection` function on only two sets. You can call it on as many sets as you like. This code finds the common elements of four sets:

```
(s1.intersection(s2, s3, s4))
```

Vocabulary

list: An abstract data type that describes a data structure that stores ordered values.

array: A data structure that stores elements with indexes in a contiguous block of memory.

homogeneous data structure: A data structure that can store elements of only a single data type, such as integer or float.

heterogeneous variable-length array: An array whose size can change after you create it that can also store multiple data types.

variable-length array: An array that's size can change after you create it.

heterogeneous array: An array that can hold different types of data.

base address: The memory location of the first element in an array.

one-dimensional array: An array where you access each element in the array by an integer index.

multidimensional array: An array where you access each element using an index tuple.

overallocation: Reserving more memory for a list than what it would strictly need and keeping track of how many elements the list is storing and how much unused space the list has.

set: A data structure that cannot contain duplicate elements.

Challenge

1. Given an array called `an_array` of non-negative integers, return an array consisting of all the even elements of `an_array`, followed by all the odd elements of `an_array`.

10 Linked Lists

*Learning to write programs stretches your mind and helps you think better [and] creates
a way of thinking about things that I think is helpful in all domains.*

Bill Gates, Co-founder, Microsoft

A **linked list** is another implementation of the list abstract data type. Like an array, you can append, prepend, search for, and delete items in a linked list. However, elements in a linked list do not have indexes because your computer does not store the items in a linked list in sequential memory locations. Instead, a linked list contains a chain of **nodes**, with each node holding a piece of data and the next node's location in the chain. The data in each node that stores the next node's location in the linked list is called a **pointer**. The first node in a linked list is called the **head**. The last element in a linked list often contains a pointer that points to None, so you know it is the last node in the list (Figure 10.1).

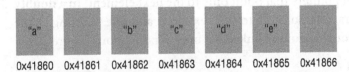

Figure 10.1: A linked list is a chain of nodes.

Unlike an array, your computer can store the nodes in a linked list in nonconsecutive memory locations (Figure 10.2).

"a"	"b"	"c"	"d"	"e"	
0x41860	0x41861	0x41862	0x41863	0x41864	0x41865	0x41866

Figure 10.2: A linked list does not need to store nodes
in consecutive memory locations.

In Figure 10.2, your computer stores the character *a* at the memory location 41860. Your computer does not have to store the next element in the list, *b*, at the next sequential memory location (41861). Instead, your computer can store *b* anywhere in memory. In this case, your computer is storing it at memory location 41862.

Each node carries a pointer to the next node's address in the list, connecting all the list elements (Figure 10.3). The first element in the linked list, *a*, carries a pointer to memory address 1862, which is the location of *b*, the second element in the list. The element *b* contains a pointer to the location of the next node's memory address, *c*, etc. This design creates a sequence of elements that are all mapped together.

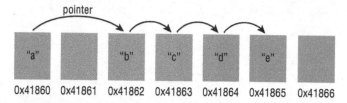

Figure 10.3: Pointers map the nodes of a linked list.

When you insert an element into a linked list, your computer does not have to shift any data because it has to adjust only two pointers. For example, Figure 10.4 shows what happens when you add the element *f* into your list after *a*.

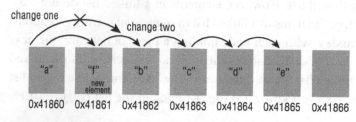

Figure 10.4: Inserting an element into a linked list requires adjusting two pointers.

Your computer changes the pointer for *a* to the memory location of *f* and adds a pointer in *f* to the next item, *b* (see Figure 10.4). Nothing else needs to change.

There are many different types of linked lists. The linked list in Figure 10.4 is singly linked. A **singly linked list** is a type of linked list with pointers that point only to the next element. In a **doubly linked list**, each node contains two pointers: one pointing to the next node and one pointing to the previous node. This allows you to move through a doubly linked list in either direction (Figure 10.5).

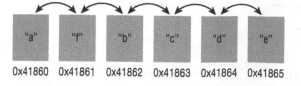

Figure 10.5: A doubly linked list has pointers that go in two directions.

You can iterate through a singly linked list only by starting at the head and moving to the end. You can iterate through a doubly linked list from the head to the end, but you can also go backward between nodes.

In a **circular linked list**, the last node points back to the first node, which allows you to go from the last element of the list back to the front of the list (Figure 10.6). This type of data structure is useful in applications that repeatedly cycle through data that doesn't have a clear beginning or ending point. For example, you could use a circular linked list to track players in a round-robin online game, or you could use a circular list in a resource pooling environment where users take turns using allocated slices of CPU time. A linked list contains a **cycle** when any node points back to a previous node.

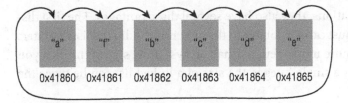

Figure 10.6: A circular linked list points from the end back to the head.

Linked List Performance

In an array, you can access an item in constant time if you know its index. However, the only way to access an element in a linked list is to do a linear search for it, which is $O(n)$ (Figure 10.7). Adding and removing a node in a linked list, on the other hand, is $O(1)$, whereas inserting and deleting items from an array is $O(n)$. This difference is the most significant advantage of using a linked list over an array. Finally, searching a linked list, like an array, is also $O(n)$.

Data Structure	Time Complexity							
	Average				Worst			
	Access	Search	Insertion	Deletion	Access	Search	Insertion	Deletion
Array	$O(1)$	$O(n)$	$O(n)$	$O(n)$	$O(1)$	$O(n)$	$O(n)$	$O(n)$
Stack	$O(n)$	$O(n)$	$O(1)$	$O(1)$	$O(n)$	$O(n)$	$O(1)$	$O(1)$
Queue	$O(n)$	$O(n)$	$O(1)$	$O(1)$	$O(n)$	$O(n)$	$O(1)$	$O(1)$
Linked List	$O(n)$	$O(n)$	$O(1)$	$O(1)$	$O(n)$	$O(n)$	$O(1)$	$O(1)$
Hash Table	N/A	$O(1)$	$O(1)$	$O(1)$	N/A	$O(n)$	$O(n)$	$O(n)$
Binary Search Tree	$O(\log n)$	$O(\log n)$	$O(\log n)$	$O(\log n)$	$O(n)$	$O(n)$	$O(n)$	$O(n)$

Figure 10.7: Linked list operation run times

Conceptually, a linked list is the same as a Python list or array, and you can use a linked list in any situation you would use them. As you know, adding or removing data from an array is $O(n)$, so you should consider using one if you're writing an algorithm that adds and removes data often because adding data to a linked list is $O(1)$. Memory management systems in operating systems use linked lists extensively, as do databases, and business systems for accounting, financial transactions, and sales transactions. You can also use a linked list to create other data structures. For example, you can use a linked list to create two data structures you will learn about in later chapters: stacks and queues. Finally, linked lists are essential to the blockchain technology behind the web 3.0 movement, which powers cryptocurrency. Blockchains themselves are similar to linked lists, and some blockchains use linked lists in their technology.

While linked lists are useful in some situations, they also have several disadvantages. The first disadvantage of a linked list is that each node must carry a pointer to the next node. A linked list's pointers require system resources, so linked lists require more memory than arrays. If the size of the data you are storing in a single node is small, such as a single integer, the size of a linked list can be twice the size of an array holding the same data.

The second disadvantage of a linked list is that it does not allow random access. In computer science, **random access** is when you can access data randomly in constant time. For example, there is no way to jump to the third element in a linked list like you could in an array. Instead, you have to start at the head of the list and follow each pointer until you reach the third element. While this can be a disadvantage, there are some more advanced versions of linked lists that overcome this problem.

Create a Linked List

There are many different ways to implement a linked list in Python. One way to create a linked list is to define classes representing the linked list and its nodes. Here is how you define a class to represent a node:

```
class Node:
    def __init__(self, data, next=None):
        self.data = data
        self.next = next
```

Your class has two variables: the first, data, holds a piece of data, and the second, next, contains the next node in the list. In Python, you don't have to deal directly with memory addresses (like in the programming language C) because it handles that for you. When you create an object, like an instance of a class called Node, Python returns a pointer (or reference) to the object. This pointer is, essentially, an address of where the actual data resides in the computer's memory. When you assign objects to variables in Python, you are dealing with pointers (references), so you can easily link objects together because Python is doing all the underlying work for you.

Next, you define a class to represent your linked list, with an instance variable called `head` that holds your list's head:

```
class LinkedList:
    def __init__(self):
        self.head = None
```

Inside your `LinkedList` class, you create an append method that adds a new node to your list:

```
class LinkedList:
    def __init__(self):
        self.head = None

    def append(self, data):
        if not self.head:
            self.head = Node(data)
            return
        current = self.head
        while current.next:
            current = current.next
        current.next = Node(data)
```

Your method `append` accepts a piece of data as a parameter, creates a new node with it, and adds it to your linked list.

If your list doesn't have a head yet, you create a new node, and it becomes the head of your linked list:

```
if not self.head:
    self.head = Node(data)
    return
```

Otherwise, if your list already has a head, you find the last node in your linked list, create a new node, and set its instance variable *next* to it. To accomplish this, you create a variable called `current` and assign it to your list's head:

```
current = self.head
```

Then you use a `while` loop that continues as long as `current.next` is not `None` because you know you are at the end of your linked list when it is:

```
while current.next:
```

Inside your `while` loop, you continually assign `current` to `current.next` until `current` is `None` (and you've reached the end of your list), and your `while` loop terminates:

```
while current.next:
    current = current.next
```

The variable `current` now holds the last node in your list, so you create a new node and assign it to `current.next`:

```
current.next = Node(data)
```

Here is an example of using `append` to add new nodes to your linked list:

```
a_list = LinkedList()
a_list.append("Tuesday")
a_list.append("Wednesday")
```

You can also add the `__str__` method to your `LinkedList` class so you can easily print all of the nodes in your list:

```
def __str__ (self):
    node = self.head
    while node is not None:
        print(node.data)
        node = node.next


a_list = LinkedList()
a_list.append("Tuesday")
a_list.append("Wednesday")
print(a_list)

>> Tuesday
>> Wednesday
```

In Python, `__str__` is a "magic method." When you define `__str__` inside a class, Python calls that method when you print the object.

While Python does not have linked lists built into the language, it does have a built-in data structure called a *deque*, which uses linked lists internally. Using Python's built-in deque data structure allows you to take advantage of a linked list's efficiency without having to code one yourself.

```
from collections import deque


d = deque()
d.append('Harry')
d.append('Potter')

for item in d:
    print(item)

>> 'Harry'
>> 'Potter'
```

Search a Linked List

You can slightly modify your `append` method from your `LinkedList` class in the previous section to search for an item in a linked list:

```
def search(self, target):
    current = self.head
    while current.next:
        if current.data == target:
            return True
        else:
            current = current.next
    return False
```

Your method, called `search`, accepts one parameter called `target`, which is the piece of data you are looking for. You iterate through your linked list, and if the current node's data matches the target value, you return `True`:

```
if current.data == target:
    return True
```

If the current node's data is not a match, you set `current` to the next node in the linked list and continue iterating:

```
else:
    current = current.next
```

If you reach the end of your linked list without a match, you know it is not in your list and return `False`:

```
return False
```

You can see this algorithm in action by creating a linked list of 20 random numbers with values ranging from 1 to 30 and searching it for the number 10:

```
import random

a_list = LinkedList()

for i in range(0, 20):
    j = random.randint(1, 30)
    a_list.append(j)
    print(j, end= " ")
```

Removing a Node from a Linked List

Removing a node from a linked list is another common technical interview question. You can also use a linear search to find a node in a linked list and delete it. You delete a node by changing the previous node's pointer so it no longer points to the node you want to delete (Figure 10.8).

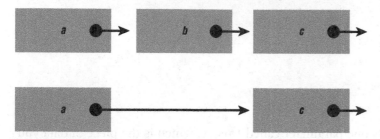

Figure 10.8: To remove a node, change the previous node's pointer.

Here is how to remove a node from a linked list:

```
def remove(self, target):
    if self.head == target:
        self.head = self.head.next
        return
    current = self.head
    previous = None
    while current:
        if current.data == target:
            previous.next = current.next
        previous = current
        current = current.next
```

Your method `remove` accepts one parameter, `target`, which is the piece of data that the node you want to remove contains.

Inside your method, first you handle what happens if the node you want to delete is the head of your list:

```
if self.head == target:
    self.head = self.head.next
    return
```

If it is, you set `self.head` to the next node in your list and return.

Otherwise, you iterate through your linked list, keeping track of both the current node and the previous node in the variables `current` and `previous`:

```
current = self.head
previous = None
```

Next, you use a `while` loop to iterate through your linked list. If you find the data you are looking for, you set `previous.next` to `current.next`, which removes the node from your list:

```
while current:
    if current.data == target:
        previous.next = current.next
    previous = current
    current = current.next
```

Reverse a Linked List

You should also know how to reverse a linked list. To reverse a linked list, you iterate through the list, keeping track of both the current node and the previous node. Then, you make the current node point to the previous node. Once you've changed all the pointers in your linked list, you've reversed it (Figure 10.9).

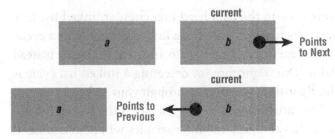

Figure 10.9: Reversing a linked list

Let's take a look at the code to reverse a linked list:

```
def reverse_list(self):
    current = self.head
    previous = None
    while current:
        next = current.next
        current.next = previous
        previous = current
        current = next
    self.head = previous
```

First, you use a `while` loop to iterate through your linked list, using the variables `current` and `previous` to keep track of the current node and the previous node.

Inside your `while` loop, first you assign `current.next` to the variable `next` so that you save that data when you assign `current.next` to `previous` in the next line. Once you've set `current.next` to `previous`, you've reversed the pointer for that node.

```
next = current.next
current.next = previous
```

Then, all you have to do is set `previous` to `current` and set `current` to `next` to continue iterating through your linked list and changing the rest of the pointers:

```
previous = current
current = next
```

Once you've changed all your pointers, you set `self.head` to `previous`. The reason you set the head to `previous` and not `current` is because once you've made it to the end of your linked list, `current` will be `None`, and `previous` will contain what used to be the last node in your linked list, which you turn into the first node when you set it to your list's head.

Finding a Linked List Cycle

Earlier, you learned that the last element points back to the list's head in a circular linked list (see Figure 10.6). Another common interview question is to detect whether a linked list contains a cycle. In other words, you are checking whether the last item in the list points to any item in the list instead of having `None` as its value for its "next" variable. One algorithm for detecting a linked list cycle is called the *tortoise-and-the-hare algorithm*. In the algorithm, you iterate through your linked list at two different speeds, keeping track of nodes in a `slow` variable and a `fast` variable. If the linked list is a circle, eventually the `fast` variable will lap the `slow` variable, and both variables will be the same. If that happens, you know the linked list is circular. If you reach the end of your linked list without it happening, you know it does not contain a cycle.

Here is how you implement a tortoise-and-the-hare algorithm:

```
def detect_cycle(self):
    slow = self.head
    fast = self.head
    while True:
        try:
            slow = slow.next
            fast = fast.next.next
            if slow is fast:
                return True
        except:
            return False
```

You start with two variables, a fast variable and a slow variable:

```
slow = self.head
fast = self.head
```

Then you create an infinite loop:

```
while True:
```

Inside your infinite loop, you assign the next node in the linked list to slow and the node after it to fast. You put this code inside a try block because if the linked list is not circular, eventually fast will be None, which means you will call fast.next.next on None, which will cause an error. The try block also prevents your program from failing if the input is an empty list or a noncircular list with one item.

```
try:
    slow = slow.next
    fast = fast.next.next
```

Next, you check to see whether slow and fast are the same object. You are not checking whether the two linked list node's values are the same because the same data could appear in more than one node. Instead, you use the is keyword to check whether the two nodes are the same object. If they are the same object, you return True because the linked list is circular.

```
if slow is fast:
    return True
```

If there is an error, it means you called .next.next on None, which means your linked list is not circular, and you return False.

Vocabulary

linked list: An implementation of the list abstract data type.

node: A part of a data structure that contains a piece of data and can connect to other pieces of data.

pointer: The piece of data in each node that contains the location of the next node in a linked list.

head: The first node in a linked list.

singly linked list: A type of linked list with pointers that point only to the next element.

doubly linked list: A type of linked list where each node contains two pointers: one pointing to the next node and one pointing to the previous node, which allows you to move through a doubly linked list in either direction.

circular linked list: A type of linked list where the last node points back to the first node, which allows you to go from the last element of the list back to the front of the list.

cycle: When any node in a linked list points back to a previous node.

random access: When you can access data randomly in constant time.

Challenges

1. Create a linked list that holds the numbers from 1 to 100. Then, print every node in your list.
2. Create two linked lists: one that contains a cycle and one that doesn't. Make sure each one has a detect_cycle method to see if it has a cycle. Call detect_cycle on each list.

11 Stacks

If you want to create and be a visionary, you're probably going to be working with technology in some way.

Steph Curry

A **stack** is an abstract data type and a linear data structure that allows you to remove only the most recent element you added. You can imagine a stack as a pile of books or dishes. In a pile of books, you can add or remove only the top book. To reach the third book in a pile of books, you must first remove all the books above it.

A stack is an example of a last-in, first-out (LIFO) data structure. A **last-in, first-out data structure** is a data structure where the last item you put into the data structure is the first item to come out of it. Because you can access its contents one by one only, a stack is also an example of a **limited-access data structure**: a type of data structure that forces you to access its information in a particular order.

Stacks have two primary operations: pushing and popping (Figure 11.1). **Pushing** an item onto a stack means putting a new item in it. **Popping** an item from a stack means removing the last item from it. Stacks can also have additional operations, such as **peeking**, which means looking at the top element in a stack without removing it.

Stacks can be bounded or unbounded. A **bounded stack** is a stack that limits how many items you can add to it, while an **unbounded stack** is a stack that does not limit how many elements you can add to it. If you are still confused about the difference between an abstract data type and a data structure, a stack might help you understand the difference. The stack abstract data type describes the idea of a data structure that only allows you to access the most recent item you put on it. However, there are several different ways to create a data structure like this. For example, you can create a stack by defining a class that internally uses either a linked list or an array to track the stack's items. When you are writing the code for a stack using either an array or a linked list, you've moved from the abstract idea of a stack to a data structure: the actual implementation of an abstract data type.

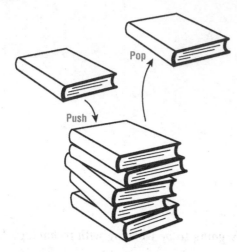

Figure 11.1: Data can be pushed on a stack or popped from it.

When to Use Stacks

Pushing and popping elements from a stack are all O(1). While stacks are efficient for adding and removing data, they are not as efficient for operations that require you to access the entire stack (Figure 11.2). For example, suppose you needed to print the contents of a stack. One solution is to print each object as you pop it off the stack. Printing each element as it comes off your stack is O(n). However, it also produces a list of objects in reverse order. Your stack will also be empty because you've popped all the items off of it. Another solution is to pop each element off the original stack as you append them to a temporary stack. Then you can print each element as you pop it off the temporary stack and append it back to the original stack. However, this solution requires more resources because you have to store all your data in a temporary stack. This solution is also O(2*n): twice as long as it takes to print the items in an array.

Data Structure	Time Complexity							
	Average				Worst			
	Access	Search	Insertion	Deletion	Access	Search	Insertion	Deletion
Array	O(1)	O(n)	O(n)	O(n)	O(1)	O(n)	O(n)	O(n)
Stack	O(n)	O(n)	O(1)	O(1)	O(n)	O(n)	O(1)	O(1)
Queue	O(n)	O(n)	O(1)	O(1)	O(n)	O(n)	O(1)	O(1)
Linked List	O(n)	O(n)	O(1)	O(1)	O(n)	O(n)	O(1)	O(1)
Hash Table	N/A	O(1)	O(1)	O(1)	N/A	O(n)	O(n)	O(n)
Binary Search Tree	O(log n)	O(log n)	O(log n)	O(log n)	O(n)	O(n)	O(n)	O(n)

Figure 11.2: Stack operation run times

Stacks are one of the most frequently used data structures in computing. Computer scientists use stacks to implement breadth-first search algorithms to search for data in trees and graphs (which you will learn about in later chapters). The run-time systems for languages like Python and Java use a stack internally to handle function calls. Compilers use stacks to parse expressions, especially when you have expressions that use nested pairs of parentheses, like in standard arithmetic expressions, or nested pairs of brackets or braces. Computer scientists also use stacks in the backtracking algorithms you find in machine learning and other artificial intelligence areas. Because adding and removing elements from a stack are both O(1), they are an excellent choice whenever you are adding and removing data elements often. For example, programs that need an "undo" mechanism often use a stack or two to handle both "undo" and "redo." Web browsers, for instance, often use two stacks to move backward and forward through your browsing history. Because accessing every element in a stack is O(n), they are not the best choice for algorithms that need to access every piece of data in a data collection continually.

Creating a Stack

As you have learned, there are a few ways to use a stack in Python. One way is to create a `Stack` class and manage its data internally using an array:

```python
class Stack:
    def __init__(self):
        self.items = []

    def push(self, data):
        self.items.append(data)

    def pop(self):
        return self.items.pop()

    def size(self):
        return len(self.items)

    def is_empty(self):
        return len(self.items) == 0

    def peek(self):
        return self.items[-1]
```

Inside your `Stack` class's __init__ method, you define an instance variable called `items` and set it to an empty list. This list is where you will keep track of the items in your stack.

```python
class Stack:
    def __init__(self):
        self.items = []
```

Next, you define your stack's `push` method. You use Python's built-in `append` method to add a new piece of data to the end of `items`:

```
def push(self, data):
    self.items.append(data)
```

Your stack's next method is `pop`. Inside `pop`, you use Python's built-in `pop` method to return the most recently added item in your stack:

```
def pop(self):
    return self.items.pop()
```

The next method in your `Stack` class is called `size`, and it uses the `len` method to return the length of your stack:

```
def size(self):
    return len(self.items)
```

Your method `is_empty` checks whether your stack is empty:

```
def is_empty(self):
    return len(self.items) == 0
```

Finally, your last method is called `peek` and returns the last item in your stack.

```
def peek(self):
    return self.items[-1]
```

You can also implement a `Stack` class by using a linked list internally. Here's how to create a simple stack (with just push and pop) using a linked list:

```
class Node:
    def __init__(self, data):
        self.data = data
        self.next = None


class Stack:
    def __init__(self):
        self.head = None

    def push(self, data):
        node = Node(data)
        if self.head is None:
            self.head = node
        else:
            node.next = self.head
```

```
            self.head = node

    def pop(self):
        if self.head is None:
            raise IndexError('pop from empty stack')
        poppednode = self.head
        self.head = self.head.next
        return poppednode.data
```

First, you define a node class to represent the nodes in your stack's internal linked list:

```
class Node:
    def __init__(self, data):
        self.data = data
        self.next = None
```

Inside your Stack class, you define an instance variable for your linked list's head:

```
class Stack:
    def __init__(self):
        self.head = None
```

Next, you define a method called push. Inside push, you create a new node. If your linked list doesn't have a head, you assign it to the new node. Otherwise, you make this node the head of your linked list.

```
def push(self, data):
    node = Node(data)
    if self.head is None:
        self.head = node
    else:
        node.next = self.head
        self.head = node
```

Then, you define a method called pop:

```
def pop(self):
    if self.head is None:
        raise IndexError('pop from empty stack')
    poppednode = self.head
    self.head = self.head.next
    return poppednode.data
```

If someone tries to pop from your stack when it's empty, you raise an exception:

```
if self.head is None:
    raise IndexError('pop from empty stack')
```

Otherwise, you remove the first item in your linked list and return it:

```
poppednode = self.head
self.head = self.head.next
return poppednode.data
```

Here is an example of creating a stack using this code and pushing and popping items on and off of it:

```
stack = Stack()
stack.push(1)
stack.push(2)
stack.push(3)

for i in range(3):
    print(stack.pop())

>> 3
>> 2
>> 1
```

Finally, you can also use a Python list as a stack. Here is how it works:

```
stack = []
print(stack)
stack.append('Kanye West')
print(stack)
stack.append('Jay-Z')
print(stack)
stack.append('Chance the Rapper')
print(stack)
stack.pop()
print(stack)

>> []
>> ['Kanye West']
>> ['Kanye West', 'Jay-Z']
>> ['Kanye West', 'Jay-Z', 'Chance the Rapper']
>> ['Kanye West', 'Jay-Z']
```

Python's lists come with the methods `append` and `pop`. The `append` method adds an item to the end of a list, which is the same as pushing an item onto a stack. The `pop` method removes an item from the end of a list. If you don't specify which item to remove, it removes the last item.

When you first print your stack, it is empty because you haven't added anything to it yet.

```
>> []
```

Next, you push three items—`'Kanye West'`, `'Jay-Z'`, and `'Chance the Rapper'`—onto your stack with these lines of code:

```
stack.append('Kanye West')
stack.append('Jay-Z')
stack.append('Chance the Rapper')
```

Then, you pop the last element, `'Chance the Rapper'`, off your stack, leaving the first two elements:

```
stack.pop()
```

That is why when you print your stack for the final time, `'Chance the Rapper'` is missing:

```
>> ['Kanye West', 'Jay-Z']
```

Of course, when you use a Python list as a stack, you are not limited to taking items off your stack in the order you put them on, so if you want to enforce that, you need to create a `Stack` class.

Using Stacks to Reverse Strings

A common interview question for Python jobs is to reverse a string three different ways. If you are familiar with Python, you know you can reverse a string like this:

```
a_string[::-1]
```

or like this:

```
''.join(reversed('a string'))
```

When it comes to reversing a string a third way, you may be stuck, however. The key is what you learned earlier in this chapter: you can use a stack to reverse a string because when you pop characters off a stack, they come off the stack in reverse order (see Figure 11.3).

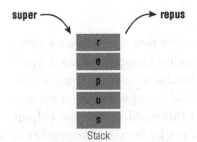

Figure 11.3: If you pop off the characters of `super`, you get `repus`.

Here is how to use a stack to reverse a string:

```
def reverse_string(a_string):
    stack = []
    string = ""
    for c in a_string:
        stack.append(c)
    for c in a_string:
        string += stack.pop()
    return string

print(reverse_string("Bieber"))

>> "rebeiB"
```

Your function `reverse_string` accepts a string as a parameter:

```
def reverse_string(a_string):
```

Inside your function, you use a `for` loop to push each character onto your stack:

```
for c in a_string:
    stack.append(c)
```

You then use another loop to iterate through your stack and add each character to your `a_string` variable as you pop them off your stack:

```
for c in a_string:
    string += stack.pop()
```

Finally, you return your reversed string:

```
return string
```

Min Stack

Another common technical interview challenge is to design a data structure that supports stack operations such as push and pop and includes a method to return the smallest element. All stack operations must be O(1). The key to solving this challenge is to use two stacks: a main stack and a min stack. Your main stack will keep track of all the push and pop operations, and your min stack will keep track of the smallest element in the stack. Learning how to solve this problem isn't just helpful for passing a technical interview: learning how to create a stack that tracks the smallest number is helpful in various situations you will encounter in your day-to-day programming.

Here is how to implement a stack that keeps track of the minimum element in Python:

```python
class MinStack():
    def __init__(self):
        self.main = []
        self.min = []

    def push(self, n):
        if len(self.main) == 0:
            self.min.append(n)
        elif n <= self.min[-1]:
            self.min.append(n)
        else:
            self.min.append(self.min[-1])
        self.main.append(n)

    def pop(self):
        self.min.pop()
        return self.main.pop()

    def get_min(self):
        return self.min[-1]
```

First, you define a class called MinStack. Inside __init__, you define two instance variables: main and min. You assign both variables to empty lists. You will use main to keep track of your main stack and use min to keep track of the smallest element.

```python
class MinStack():
    def __init__(self):
        self.main = []
        self.min = []
```

Next, you define your stack's push method. Inside push, you check to see whether self.main is empty because if it is, then no matter what n is, it is the smallest number in your stack. If self.main is empty, you append n to min.

```python
def push(self, n):
    if len(self.main) == 0:
        self.min.append(n)
```

If self.main is not empty, you check to see whether n is less than or equal to the last item in self.min. The last item in self.min always needs to be the smallest number in your stack, so if n is less than or equal to the last item in self.min, you append n to self.min.

```python
elif n <= self.min[-1]:
    self.min.append(n)
```

If n is not less than or equal to the last item in self.min (and is, therefore, larger), you append the last item in self.min to self.min:

```
else:
    self.min.append(self.min[-1])
```

Appending the last item in self.min to self.min keeps the number of items in self.main the same as self.min so that you can keep track of the smallest number in the stack.

Let's take a look at an example. When you push the first number onto your stack, your two internal stacks look like this:

```
min_stack = MinStack()
min_stack.push(10)
print(min_stack.main)
print(min_stack.min)
>> [10]
>> [10]
```

Here's what happens when you push another, bigger number onto your stack:

```
min_stack.push(15)
print(min_stack.main)
print(min_stack.min)

>> [10, 15]
>> [10, 10]
```

Notice that min_stack.main is a normal stack, holding items in the order they come onto it:

```
>> [10, 15]
```

However, min_stack.min does not keep track of the items as they come onto the stack. Instead, it keeps track of whatever the smallest number is. In this case, it has 10 twice:

```
>> [10, 10]
```

Fifteen is not in min_stack.min because 15 will never be the smallest item in the stack.

When you call get_min, it returns the last item in self.min, which is the smallest number in the stack:

```
print(min_stack.get_min())

>> 10
```

In this case, it returns 10.

After you've popped an item, your two stacks look like this:

```
min_stack.pop()
print(min_stack.main)
print(min_stack.min)

>> [10]
>> [10]
```

And when you call `get_min` a second time, the method once again returns 10:

```
print(min_stack.get_min())
>> 10
```

When you call `pop` one last time, both stacks are empty:

```
min_stack.pop()
print(min_stack.main)
print(min_stack.min)

>> []
>> []
```

As you can see, `self.min` kept track of the smallest number in the stack without ever having to store the number 15.

Stacked Parentheses

One time, when I was interviewing at a startup, they gave me the following problem: "Given a string, use a stack to check whether it has balanced parentheses, meaning every time there is an open parenthesis, there is a subsequently closed parenthesis."

```
(str(1)) # Balanced
print(Hi!)) # Not balanced
```

Unfortunately, I messed up my answer badly. Your initial reaction to this problem may be to quickly solve it by parsing a string while using one counter for opening parentheses and another counter for closing parentheses. If the counters are equal at the end of the string, then the parentheses are balanced. However, what happens if you encounter a string like the following one?

```
a_string = ")( )("
```

In this case, your solution will not work.

A better way to solve this problem is to use a stack. First, you iterate through each character in the string, and if a parenthesis is open, you put it on the stack. If it is closed, you check to see whether an open parenthesis is already on the stack. If there isn't, it means the string is not balanced. If there is, you pop an open parenthesis off the stack. If there are an equal number of opening and closing parentheses in the string, the stack will be empty at the end of your loop. If the stack is not empty, then there are not equal numbers of opening and closing parentheses.

Let's check out the code:

```
def check_parentheses(a_string):
    stack = []
    for c in a_string:
        if c == "(":
            stack.append(c)
        if c == ")":
            if len(stack) == 0:
                return False
            else:
                stack.pop()
    return len(stack) == 0
```

Your `check_parentheses` function accepts the string to check for balanced parentheses as a parameter:

```
def check_parentheses(a_string):
```

Inside your function, you create a stack using a list:

```
stack = []
```

You use a `for` loop to iterate through the characters in `a_string`:

```
for c in a_string:
```

If the character is an opening parenthesis, you push it onto your stack:

```
if c == "(":
    stack.append(c)
```

If the symbol is a closing parenthesis and the stack is empty, you return `False` because there is no matching opening parenthesis on your stack, which means the string is not balanced. If there are opening parentheses in the stack, you pop one off to match the closing parenthesis.

```
if c == ")":
    if len(stack) == 0:
        return False
    else:
        stack.pop()
```

Once your `for` loop finishes, you return whether or not the length of your stack is zero:

```
return len(stack) == 0
```

If your function returns `True`, the parentheses are balanced; otherwise, they are not.

Understanding how to solve this problem is not just useful for technical interviews. The compilers for languages like Python and Java have code like this for parsing and evaluating expressions. If you ever need to write your own programming language or write code to parse data with opening and closing symbols, you can write code like this to evaluate it.

Vocabulary

stack: An abstract data type and a linear data structure that allows you to remove only the most recent element you added.

last in, first out data structure: A data structure where the last item you put into the data structure is the first item to come out of it.

limited-access data structure: A type of data structure that forces you to access its information in a particular order.

pushing: Putting a new item onto a stack.

popping: Removing the last item from a stack.

peeking: Looking at the top element in a stack without removing it.

bounded stack: A stack that limits how many items you can add to it.

unbounded stack: A stack that does not limit how many items you can add to it.

Challenges

1. Modify your balanced string program to check whether both parentheses, ( ), and brackets, { }, are balanced in a string.
2. Design a max stack that allows you to push, pop, and keep track of your stack's biggest number in $O(1)$ time.

Queues

All students should have the opportunity to learn how to program. Computer science is the basis for modern day creativity and expression. The computer programmers of tomorrow will revolutionize medicine.

Anne Wojcicki

A **queue** is an abstract data type and a linear data structure where you can add items only to the rear and remove them from the front (Figure 12.1). The queue abstract data type describes a data structure that works like the checkout lines at a grocery store: the first person in the line is the first person to check out, and newcomers join the line's rear.

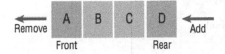

Figure 12.1: In a queue, you add items to the rear and remove them from the front.

A queue is an example of a first-in, first-out (FIFO) data structure. As the name implies, in a **first-in, first-out data structure**, the first item to enter the data structure is the first to come out of it. Queues, like stacks, are limited access data structures.

Queues have two primary operations: enqueueing and dequeueing (Figure 12.2). **Enqueueing** means adding an item to a queue, whereas **dequeueing** means removing an item. You enqueue elements to the rear of a queue and dequeue them from the front.

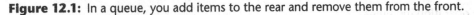
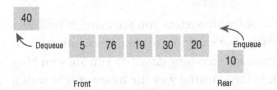

Figure 12.2: The primary operations of queues are enqueueing and dequeueing.
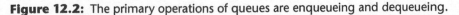

There are several different ways to implement the queue abstract data type as a data structure. For example, like with stacks, you can implement a queue data structure using an array or a linked list. Also, like stacks, queues can be bounded or unbounded. A **bounded queue** is one that limits how many items you can add to it, while an **unbounded queue** is one that does not limit how many items you can add to it. You can create a bounded queue using an array or an unbounded one using a linked list (you can also implement a bounded queue using a linked list if you keep track of the number of items you've stored in the queue).

When to Use Queues

Like stacks, queues are efficient for adding or removing data (Figure 12.3). Enqueueing and dequeueing are both O(1) regardless of the queue's size. Like stacks, queues are not efficient for accessing individual pieces of data because you have to iterate through a queue's elements to find an item. That means accessing an item in a queue and searching a queue are both O(n).

Data Structure	Time Complexity							
	Average				Worst			
	Access	Search	Insertion	Deletion	Access	Search	Insertion	Deletion
Array	O(1)	O(n)	O(n)	O(n)	O(1)	O(n)	O(n)	O(n)
Stack	O(n)	O(n)	O(1)	O(1)	O(n)	O(n)	O(1)	O(1)
Queue	O(n)	O(n)	O(1)	O(1)	O(n)	O(n)	O(1)	O(1)
Linked List	O(n)	O(n)	O(1)	O(1)	O(n)	O(n)	O(1)	O(1)
Hash Table	N/A	O(1)	O(1)	O(1)	N/A	O(n)	O(n)	O(n)
Binary Search Tree	O(log n)	O(log n)	O(log n)	O(log n)	O(n)	O(n)	O(n)	O(n)

Figure 12.3: Queue operation run times

As a programmer, you will frequently use queues. Queues are an ideal data structure when you are programming anything that relates to first come, first served. For example, a queue is helpful for programming an automated phone system that puts a caller in line when all the available operators are busy and then connects the earliest caller first, followed by callers who dialed in later. Operating systems use queues to handle requests to write data to a hard disk drive, stream audio and video, and send and receive network packets. Web servers, on the other hand, use queues to handle incoming requests.

Whenever you see a "buffering" message, it means the software system you are using is probably waiting for incoming data to add to its queue for processing. For example, to ensure smooth streaming, audio and video streaming systems often set up a queue for incoming data. Say you are watching a movie on Netflix. The software on your TV responsible for showing you the movie might wait a short amount of time before starting the movie so it can fill up its queue with the video data Netflix is sending. Once your television software allows you to start watching, more data will come in, and the system will add it to its queue. Using a queue enables the video player to take data packets off the queue's front in a fixed, constant amount of time, making the viewing experience smooth, even if the incoming data comes in at an inconsistent rate. If too many data packets come in too quickly, the system keeps the packets in the queue until it's ready for them. If the packets come in too slowly, the system can keep playing the packets in the queue until it runs out. Ideally, that doesn't happen, but when you get a "buffering" message, the queue has run out of data, and no streaming can happen until it starts to fill up again.

Let's imagine what a program like this looks like. It probably has a loop that runs until you've finished watching your program. Inside the loop, it has an algorithm. That algorithm is responsible for adding data to the queue and for removing and displaying the data to the user in the form of a video. Together, this algorithm and an appropriate data structure (a queue) are all you need to stream a movie to your television or laptop and further illustrates why programs = data structures + algorithms.

Creating a Queue

There are several different ways to implement a queue in Python. One way is to define a Queue class that uses a linked list to keep track of data internally. Here is how to create a queue using a linked list:

```python
class Node:
    def __init__(self, data, next=None):
        self.data = data
        self.next = next


class Queue:
    def __init__(self):
        self.front = None
        self.rear = None
        self._size = 0

    def enqueue(self, item):
        self._size += 1
        node = Node(item)
        if self.rear is None:
            self.front = node
            self.rear = node
        else:
            self.rear.next = node
            self.rear = node

    def dequeue(self):
        if self.front is None:
```

```
            raise IndexError('pop from empty queue')
        self._size -= 1
        temp = self.front
        self.front = self.front.next
        if self.front is None:
            self.rear = None
        return temp.data

    def size(self):
        return self._size
```

First, you define a Node class to represent the nodes in your queue's internal linked list:

```
class Node:
    def __init__(self, data, next=None):
        self.data = data
        self.next = next
```

Inside your queue, you keep track of its front and rear items in the variables self.front and self.rear. You track the front and rear of your queue so you can enqueue and dequeue in constant time. You also track your queue's size in the variable self._size.

```
def __init__(self):
    self.front = None
    self.rear = None
    self._size = 0
```

Next, you define a method called enqueue that adds an item to the rear of your queue:

```
def enqueue(self, item):
    self._size += 1
    node = Node(item)
    if self.rear is None:
        self.front = node
        self.rear = node
    else:
        self.rear.next = node
        self.rear = node
```

Your method accepts the data you want to store in your queue as a parameter:

```
def enqueue(self, item):
```

Inside enqueue, first you increment self._size by 1 because you are adding a new item to your queue. Then, you create a new node to store the item in your queue's internal linked list:

```
self._size += 1
node = Node(item)
```

If `self.rear` is `None`, it means your queue is empty, so you set `self.front` and `self.rear` to the node you just created (since there is only one item in your queue, that item is both the rear and the front). Otherwise, you assign your new node to `self.rear.next` to add it to your queue's internal linked list. Then, you assign the new node to `self.rear`, so it is at the rear of your queue.

```
if self.rear is None:
    self.front = node
    self.rear = node
else:
    self.rear.next = node
    self.rear = node
```

Next, you define a method called `dequeue` to remove an item from the front of your queue:

```
def dequeue(self):
    if self.front is None:
        raise IndexError('pop from empty queue')
    self._size -= 1
    temp = self.front
    self.front = self.front.next
    if self.front is None:
        self.rear = None
    return temp.data
```

The first line of code in your method throws an exception if you try to dequeue an item when your queue is empty:

```
if self.front is None:
    raise IndexError('pop from empty queue')
```

When you call `dequeue`, you remove and return the item at the front of your queue. To do this, you store the node at the front of your queue (`self.front`) in `temp` so you can reference it later after you remove it from your internal linked list:

```
temp = self.front
```

Next, you remove the item at the front of your queue from your queue's internal linked list by assigning `self.front` to `self.front.next`:

```
self.front = self.front.next
```

If there are no more items in your queue after you remove the item at the front of your queue, you set `self.rear` to `None` because there is no longer an item at the rear of your queue:

```
if self.front is None:
    self.rear = None
```

The last method you define is a method called `size` that returns the number of items in your queue:

```
def size(self):
    return self._size
```

With these three methods, you have created a simple queue using a linked list you can add and remove data from and check its size. You can now use your queue like this:

```
queue = Queue()
queue.enqueue(1)
queue.enqueue(2)
queue.enqueue(3)
print(queue.size())
for i in range(3):
    print(queue.dequeue())

>> 3
>> 1
>> 2
>> 3
```

In the previous code, you created a queue, added the numbers 1, 2, and 3 to it, printed your queue's size, and then printed every item in your queue.

Let's take a look at what happens inside your queue class when you run this program. When you call `enqueue`, there are no items in your queue, so you add a node to your queue's internal linked list, and it is your queue's front and rear (Figure 12.4).

```
F R
┌───┐
│ 1 │
└───┘
```

Figure 12.4: When there is one item in your queue, it is both the front and the rear.

Next, you add a 2 to your queue. Now there are two nodes in your queue's internal linked list, and the node with 1 in it is no longer the rear: the node with 2 in it is now the rear (Figure 12.5).

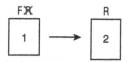

Figure 12.5: Now the node with 1 in it is the front, and the node with 2 in it is the rear.

Finally, you add a 3 to your queue. Now there are three nodes in your queue's internal linked list, and the node with 2 in it is no longer the rear: the node with 3 in it is (Figure 12.6).

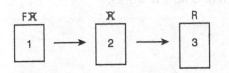

Figure 12.6: The node with 1 in it is the front, and the node with 3 in it is the rear.

When you call dequeue for the first time, your remove the node with 1 in it. Now the node with 2 in it is at the front your queue (Figure 12.7).

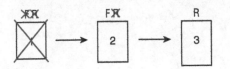

Figure 12.7: When you dequeue the 1, the front changes to the node with 2 in it.

When you call dequeue for the second time, you remove the node with 2 in it. Now the node with 3 in it is at the front and the rear of your queue (Figure 12.8).

Figure 12.8: When you dequeue again, there is only one item left, so it is both the front and the rear.

Now when you call dequeue for the third time, you remove the node with 3 in it, your queue is empty, and self.front and self.rear both point to None (Figure 12.9).

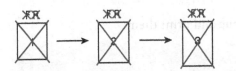

Figure 12.9: Now your queue is empty.

Python's Built-In Queue Class

Python also has a built-in class to create a queue you can use. Here is how it works:

```
from queue import Queue

q = Queue()
q.put('a')
q.put('b')
q.put('c')
print(q.qsize())
for i in range(3):
    print(q.get())

>> 3
>> a
>> b
>> c
```

First, you import `Queue` from the `queue` module:

```
from queue import Queue
```

Next, you create a queue by calling the `Queue` method:

```
q = Queue()
```

You add three strings onto your queue using the built-in method `put`:

```
q.put('a')
q.put('b')
q.put('c')
```

Then you check your queue's size using the built-in method `qsize`:

```
print(q.qsize())
```

Finally, you use a `for` loop to pop all the items off your queue and print them:

```
for i in range(3):
    print(q.get())
```

Create a Queue Using Two Stacks

A common technical interview question is to create a queue using two stacks. Here is how to do it:

```
class Queue:
    def __init__(self):
        self.s1 = []
        self.s2 = []

    def enqueue(self, item):
        while len(self.s1) != 0:
            self.s2.append(self.s1.pop())
        self.s1.append(item)
        while len(self.s2) != 0:
            self.s1.append(self.s2.pop())

    def dequeue(self):
        if len(self.s1) == 0:
            raise Exception("Cannot pop from empty queue")
        return self.s1.pop()
```

First, you define a Queue class with two internal stacks, self.s1 and self.s2:

```
class Queue:
    def __init__(self):
        self.s1 = []
        self.s2 = []
```

Next, you define a method called enqueue to add a new item to your queue:

```
def enqueue(self, item):
    while len(self.s1) != 0:
        self.s2.append(self.s1.pop())
    self.s1.append(item)
    while len(self.s2) != 0:
        self.s1.append(self.s2.pop())
```

When you add a new item to your queue, you need to put it at the rear of your first stack. Because you can add items only to the front of a stack, to put something at the rear of your first stack, you have to pop everything off it, add the new item, and then put everything back on.

In this case, you pop everything from your first stack, put it all onto your second stack, add the new item to your first stack (once it is empty), and then put everything back onto it. When you finish, your first stack will have all the original items, plus the new item at its rear.

```
while len(self.s1) != 0:
    self.s2.append(self.s1.pop())
self.s1.append(item)
while len(self.s2) != 0:
    self.s1.append(self.s2.pop())
```

Now that you've defined `enqueue`, you create a method called `dequeue` to remove an item from your queue:

```
def dequeue(self):
    if len(self.s1) == 0:
        raise Exception("Cannot pop from empty queue")
    return self.s1.pop()
```

First, you check to see whether `self.s1` is empty. If it is, it means the user is trying to `dequeue` an item from an empty queue, so you raise an exception:

```
if len(self.s1) == 0:
    raise Exception("Cannot pop from empty queue")
```

Otherwise, you pop the item at the front of your first stack and return it:

```
return self.s1.pop()
```

In this implementation of a queue, enqueueing is O(n) because you have to iterate through every item in your stack. Dequeueing, on the other hand, is O(1) because you have to remove only the last item from your internal stack.

Vocabulary

queue: A linear data structure similar to a stack.

first-in, first-out data structure: A data structure where the first item to enter the data structure is the first to come out of it.

enqueueing: Adding an item to a queue.

dequeueing: Removing an item from a queue.

bounded queue: A queue that limits how many items you can add to it.

unbounded queue: A queue that does not limit how many items you can add to it.

Challenge

1. Implement a queue using two stacks, but make enqueueing O(1).

13 Hash Tables

For self-educated scientists and thinkers such as Charles Darwin, Srinivasa Ramanujan, Leonardo da Vinci, Michael Faraday, myself, and many others, education is a relentless voyage of discovery. To us, education is an everlasting quest for knowledge and wisdom.

Abhijit Naskar

An **associative array** is an abstract data type that stores key-value pairs with unique keys. A **key-value pair** consists of two pieces of data mapped together: a key and a value. The **key** is the piece of data you use to retrieve the value. The **value** is the piece of data you use the key to retrieve. As a Python programmer, you should already be familiar with key-value pairs because you've been using Python dictionaries.

There are many different implementations of an associative array, but in this chapter, you will learn about hash tables. A **hash table** is a linear data structure that stores key-value pairs with unique keys, which means you cannot store duplicate keys in a hash table. The difference between an associative array and a hash table is that an associative array is an abstract data type, whereas a hash table is a data structure and therefore is an implementation of an associative array. Python implements dictionaries using hash tables.

When you are programming, the system you are running your program from stores the data in a hash table inside an array data structure. When you add a piece of data to your hash table, your computer uses a hash function to determine where in the array to store it. A **hash function** is code that takes a key as input and outputs an integer you can use to map a hash table key to an array index your computer uses to store the value. The index a hash function produces is called a **hash value**. You can store any type of data as a value in a hash table, but the key must be something your hash function can turn into an index, such as an integer or a string. This process makes retrieving values from a hash table incredibly efficient, which you will learn more about later.

Let's quickly review how Python dictionaries work. You store key-value pairs in a Python dictionary. Keys cannot be duplicates, but values can be. Here is an example of storing a key-value pair in a Python dictionary:

```
a_dict = {}
a_dict[1776] = 'Independence Year'
```

You can now use the key 1776 to look up the value `'Independence Year'` like this:

```
print(a_dict[1776])

>> 'Independence Year'
```

Now let's take a look at how an example hash function works by determining the location of several keys, which, in this example, will be integers. Your computer does everything you are about to see for you behind the scenes when you use a dictionary in Python. Suppose you have a hash table with seven slots, and you want to store several integers in them (Figure 13.1). (In this case, for illustrative purposes, we are dealing only with keys and not keys and their values.)

Figure 13.1: A hash table stores key-value pairs in an array.

The first number you need to store is 86. To store 86 in your hash table, you need a hash function. One simple hash function is to take each number and perform modulo by the number of slots available (Figure 13.2). For example, to get a hash value for 86, you evaluate 86 % 7. The result of 86 % 7 is 2, which means you put 86 at index two in the array you are using to store your hash table's data.

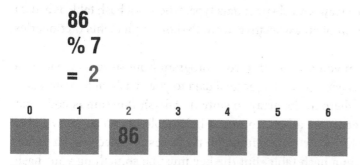

Figure 13.2: To store 86 in the hash table, you perform modulo by the number of slots and get 2.

The next number you need to put into your hash table is 90, so you evaluate 90 % 7, which is 6. So, you put 90 at index six in your array (Figure 13.3).

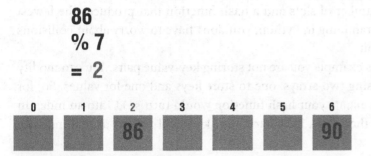

Figure 13.3: To store 90 in the hash table, you perform modulo by the number of slots and get 6.

Finally, you need to add the numbers 21, 29, 38, 39, and 40 to your hash table. Here is what happens when you use modulo 7 on these numbers:

21 % 7 = 0

29 % 7 = 1

38 % 7 = 3

39 % 7 = 4

40 % 7 = 5

When you add these numbers to your hash table, it looks like Figure 13.4.

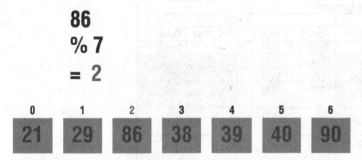

Figure 13.4: Your hash table after adding all the numbers

So far, adding data to your hash table has gone as planned. Suppose you want to add 30 to your hash table. Since 30 % 7 is 2, you should put 30 in slot 2. There is a problem, however, because 86 is already in that slot. Two numbers hashing to the same slot is a **collision**. To resolve this collision, you can place 30 in the next empty slot. That resolution works, but then when you have to find 30, you have to use a hash function to find its location in the array, look in slot 3, realize that it is not 30, and then look in subsequent slots until you find it, which adds time complexity. There are other ways of handling collisions, such as keeping lists (usually linked lists) at each location and putting each colliding pair into the list that goes with the original colliding location. When you create a hash table, your goal is to use the correct number of slots and a hash function that produces the fewest collisions. However, when you are programming in Python, you don't have to worry about collisions because dictionaries handle them for you.

As I mentioned earlier, in the previous example you are not storing key-value pairs. You can modify this example to store key-value pairs using two arrays: one to store keys and one for values. So, for example, if you were mapping `self` to `taught`, your hash function would turn `self` into an index in an array. You would then store `self` at that index in the array for keys and `taught` at that index in the array for values.

When to Use Hash Tables

Unlike the other data structures you've learned about so far (and the ones you will learn about later), on average, searching for data in a hash table is O(1). Inserting and deleting data in a hash table is O(1) on average as well. Collisions can erode the efficiency of hash tables, making searching, insertion, and deletion O(n) in the worst-case scenario. Still, hash tables are one of the most efficient structures for storing large data sets. The reason hash tables are so efficient is that to determine whether a piece of data is in a hash table, all you have to do is run your data through your hash function and check an array at that index, which is only one step. Figure 13.5 shows the run time for a hash table's operations. It does not include a run time for the Access column for hash tables because hash tables do not allow you to access the nth item in it like an array or linked list.

Data Structure	Time Complexity							
	Average				Worst			
	Access	Search	Insertion	Deletion	Access	Search	Insertion	Deletion
Array	O(1)	O(n)	O(n)	O(n)	O(1)	O(n)	O(n)	O(n)
Stack	O(n)	O(n)	O(1)	O(1)	O(n)	O(n)	O(1)	O(1)
Queue	O(n)	O(n)	O(1)	O(1)	O(n)	O(n)	O(1)	O(1)
Linked List	O(n)	O(n)	O(1)	O(1)	O(n)	O(n)	O(1)	O(1)
Hash Table	N/A	O(1)	O(1)	O(1)	N/A	O(n)	O(n)	O(n)
Binary Search Tree	O(log n)	O(log n)	O(log n)	O(log n)	O(n)	O(n)	O(n)	O(n)

Figure 13.5: Hash table operation run times

Earlier, you learned about search algorithms and how if you sort your data, you can perform a binary search, which is significantly faster than a linear search. You also learned that there was another way to search for data that is even more efficient than the binary search you will learn about later. That method is searching for data in a hash table, which is O(1), meaning that searching for data in a hash table is the fastest possible way to search for data. The ability to look up data in constant time instead of having to do a linear or binary search makes an enormous difference when working with large data sets.

As a programmer, you will frequently use hash tables. For example, if you are a web developer, you will often work with **JavaScript Object Notation (JSON)**, a data-interchange format. Many APIs send data in JSON, which you can easily turn into a Python dictionary. An **application programming interface (API)** is a program that allows applications to communicate with each other. Any time you work with a key-value database in Python, you will use dictionaries. The popular version control system Git uses the hash values from a cryptographic hash function to store different versions of the data in your projects. Operating systems often use hash tables to help manage memory. Python itself uses dictionaries (hash tables) to hold object variable names and values.

You should consider using a hash table whenever you have a large amount of data and you need to access individual data items quickly. For example, suppose you were writing a program that needed to search the English dictionary or you wanted to create an app that requires fast access to anyone's phone number in a phone book with hundreds of thousands or millions of entries. Hash tables are appropriate for either of these situations. Generally, they are a suitable data structure to use anytime you need fast, random access to data. However, if you were frequently operating on the data in sequential order, an array or a linked list might be a better choice.

Characters in a String

When you solve a problem, it is helpful to think about using a hash table in your solution because they are so efficient. For example, suppose an interviewer asks you to count all the characters in a string. One solution to this problem is to use a Python dictionary. You can store each character as a key in your dictionary and the number of times it occurs in the string as a value. Here is how it works:

```python
def count(a_string):
    a_dict = {}
    for char in a_string:
        if char in a_dict:
            a_dict[char] += 1
        else:
            a_dict[char] = 1
    print(a_dict)
```

Your function, count, accepts a string as a parameter (the string you want to count the characters of):

```python
def count(a_string):
```

Inside your function, you create a dictionary:

```python
a_dict = {}
```

Next, you use a for loop to iterate through your string:

```python
for char in a_string:
```

If the character is already in your dictionary, you increment its value by 1.

```
if char in a_dict:
    a_dict[char] += 1
```

If the character is not yet in your dictionary, you add it as a new key with a value of 1 since it is the first time the character has appeared so far.

```
else:
    a_dict[char] = 1
```

When you print your dictionary at the end, it contains each letter in the string as well as the number of times it occurs.

```
print(a_dict)
```

Let's take a look at what happens when you run your function. When you call your function and pass in the string "Hello", on the first iteration, your program will add an uppercase H as a key in your dictionary and the number 1 as its value, which means your dictionary looks like this:

```
{"H": 1}
```

On the next iteration, the character is e. Because e is not in your dictionary yet, you add it to your dictionary as a key with a value of 1. Now your dictionary looks like this:

```
{"H": 1, "e": 1}
```

You do the same thing for the letter l. Now your dictionary looks like this:

```
{"H": 1, "e": 1, "l": 1}
```

On the next iteration, the character is l again. This time, the character is already in your dictionary, so you increment its key value by 1. Now your dictionary looks like this:

```
{"H": 1, "e": 1, "l": 2}
```

This process continues until you've gone through every character in your string. When your loop is over and you print your dictionary, it looks like this:

```
{'H': 1, 'e': 1, 'l': 2, 'o': 1}
```

By taking this approach, you've not only solved this problem but solved it in $O(n)$ time by using a hash table (in this case, n is the number of characters in the string).

Two Sum

Another common technical interview question you can use a hash table to solve is called *two sum*. In the two sum challenge, an interviewer asks you to return the two numbers' indexes in an unsorted list that adds up to a target value. You can assume that only one pair adds up to the target number, and you may not use the same number in the list twice.

For example, say the target value is the number 5, and you have the following list of numbers:

```
[-1, 2, 3, 4, 7]
```

In this case, the numbers at index positions 1 and 2 add up to the target number (5), so the answer is index 1 and index 2 (2 + 3 = 5).

One way to solve this problem is to use brute force by iterating through the list and adding up each pair of numbers to see if they add up to 5. Here is how to code a brute-force solution to this problem:

```python
def two_sum_brute(the_list, target):
    index_list = []
    for i in range(0, len(the_list)):
        for j in range(i, len(the_list)):
            if the_list[i] + the_list[j] == target:
                return [the_list[i], the_list[j]]
```

Your solution uses two nested loops. Your outer loop iterates through the list of numbers using i, while your inner loop also iterates through the list using j. You use both variables to create pairs, such as –1 and 2, 2 and 3, etc., and test if they add up to the target number. Your brute-force solution is simple, but it is not efficient. Because your algorithm requires two nested loops to iterate through every combination, it is O(*n***2).

A more efficient way to solve this problem is to use a dictionary. Here is how to solve the two sum challenge using a dictionary:

```python
def two_sum(a_list, target):
    a_dict = {}
    for index, n in enumerate(a_list):
        rem = target - n
        if rem in a_dict:
            return index, a_dict[rem]
        else:
            a_dict[n] = index
```

Your function two_sum takes two arguments, a list of numbers and the target number they should add up to:

```python
def two_sum(a_list, target):
```

Inside your function, you create a dictionary:

```
a_dict = {}
```

Then, you call `enumerate` on the list, which allows you to iterate through the list while keeping track of each number and its index in the list:

```
for index, n in enumerate(a_list):
```

Next, you subtract n from the target number:

```
rem = target - n
```

The result is the number the current number needs to match with to add up to the target number you are looking for. If the number in the variable `rem` is in your dictionary, you know you've found the answer, so you return the current index and look up the index of the number you stored using the key `rem` inside your dictionary:

```
return index, a_dict[rem]
```

If the number in the variable `rem` is not in your dictionary, you add it to your dictionary, putting n as the key and its index as the value:

```
else:
    a_dict[n] = index
```

Let's take a look at how this works. Say you ran your program with this list and a target number of 5:

```
[-1, 2, 3, 4, 7]
```

The first time around your loop, n is –1 and nothing is in your dictionary, so you add –1 at index 0 to your dictionary. The second time around your loop, n is 2, so `rem` is 3 (5 – 2), so this time you add 2 at index 1 to your dictionary. The third time around your loop, n is 3, which means `rem` is 2. You already put 2 in your dictionary, which means you've found the answer.

Unlike your brute-force approach to solving your problem, this solution is $O(n)$ because using a hash table means you no longer have to use two nested `for` loops, so it is much more efficient.

Vocabulary

associative array: An abstract data type that stores key-value pairs with unique keys.

key-value pair: Two pieces of data mapped together: a key and a value.

key: The piece of data you use to retrieve the value.

value: The piece of data you use the key to retrieve.

hash table: A linear data structure that stores key-value pairs with unique keys.

hash function: Code that takes a key as input and outputs a unique piece of data that maps the key to an array index your computer uses to store the value.

hash value: The unique value a hash function produces.

collision: When two numbers hash to the same slot.

JavaScript Object Notation (JSON): A data-interchange format.

application programming interface (API): A program that allows applications to communicate with each other.

Challenge

1. Given a string, remove all duplicates words. For example, given the string
   `"I am a self-taught programmer looking for a job as a programmer."`, your function should return
   `"I am a self-taught programmer looking for a job as a."`.

Binary Trees

The most powerful people are the ones who never stop learning.

Rejoice Denhere

So far, all the data structures you've learned about have been linear. In the following chapters, you will learn about a few essential nonlinear data structures and abstract data types. The first one we will discuss is a **tree**, a nonlinear abstract data type made up of nodes connected in a hierarchical structure (Figure 14.1). Common tree operations include inserting, searching, and deleting.

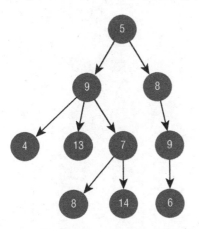

Figure 14.1: An example of a tree data structure

There are several types of tree data structures: general trees, AVL trees, red-black trees, binary trees, binary search trees, and more. In this chapter, you will learn about general trees, binary search trees, and binary trees, with an emphasis on binary trees. Although covering every type of tree is outside of the scope of this book, I encourage you to learn more about other types of trees on your own.

A general tree is a data structure that starts with a node at the top. The node at the top of a tree is called the **root node**. Each node connected underneath a node in a tree is its **child node**. A node with one or more child nodes is called a **parent node**. **Sibling nodes** share the same parent. The connection between two nodes in a tree is called an **edge** (Figure 14.2).

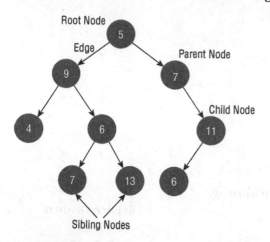

Figure 14.2: A tree with a root node, parent nodes, child nodes, and edges

You can move from one node to another as long as they share an edge (Figure 14.3).

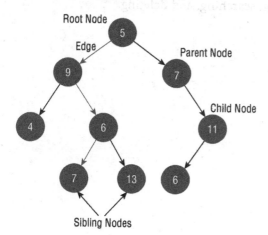

Figure 14.3: A path through a tree

Every node in a tree except the root has a single parent node. A node without child nodes is called a **leaf node**, and a node with child nodes is called a **branch node**.

A **binary tree** is a tree data structure where each node can have only two child nodes (sometimes called a *child* or *children*). Every node in a binary tree (except the root) is either the left or right child of a parent node (Figure 14.4).

Everything else in a binary tree is the same as a general tree; the only difference is the child node limit.

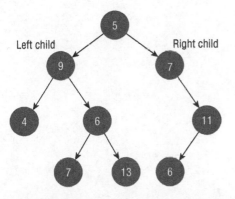

Figure 14.4: In a binary tree, a parent node can have only two child nodes.

A **binary search tree** is a tree data structure where each node can have only two children, and the tree stores its nodes in sorted order where every node's value is greater than any value in its left subtree and lower than any value in its right subtree (Figure 14.5). Like hash table keys, you cannot store duplicate values in a binary search tree. You can get around this restriction and handle duplicate values by adding a count field in your tree's node objects to track the number of occurrences of a given value.

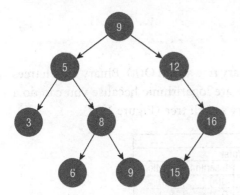

Figure 14.5: An example of a binary search tree

Unlike linear data structures like arrays and linked lists, you cannot always traverse a tree without backtracking. You can reach any node in a tree by starting from the root node, but once you have moved away from the root node, you can reach only that node's descendants. A node's **descendants** are its children and their children and their children's children, etc. For example, Figure 14.6 shows a simple tree with a root node A, leaf nodes B, D, and E, and a branch node C. The A node has two children (B and C), and the C node has two children (D and E). The nodes B, C, D, and E are the A node's descendants.

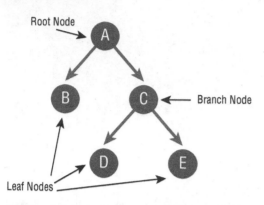

Figure 14.6: A simple tree showing the root node, A, and its descendants

If you start from the root node and move only to right child nodes, you will walk through the nodes A, C, and E. If you instead move only to left child nodes, you will walk through the nodes A and B. You may have noticed that neither of these traversals includes the node D. To get to the node D, you must first move to the A node's right child and then the C node's left child. In other words, to get to the D node in this binary tree, you have to backtrack.

When to Use Trees

Inserting, deleting, and searching for data in a general and binary tree are all $O(n)$. Binary search trees are more efficient: all three operations in a binary search tree are logarithmic because you can do a binary search to insert, delete, and search for nodes in a binary search tree (Figure 14.7).

Data Structure	Time Complexity							
	Average				Worst			
	Access	Search	Insertion	Deletion	Access	Search	Insertion	Deletion
Array	O(1)	O(n)	O(n)	O(n)	O(1)	O(n)	O(n)	O(n)
Stack	O(n)	O(n)	O(1)	O(1)	O(n)	O(n)	O(1)	O(1)
Queue	O(n)	O(n)	O(1)	O(1)	O(n)	O(n)	O(1)	O(1)
Linked List	O(n)	O(n)	O(1)	O(1)	O(n)	O(n)	O(1)	O(1)
Hash Table	N/A	O(1)	O(1)	O(1)	N/A	O(n)	O(n)	O(n)
Binary Search Tree	O(log n)	O(log n)	O(log n)	O(log n)	O(n)	O(n)	O(n)	O(n)

Figure 14.7: Binary search trees operation run times

You may be wondering why, if every operation is linear, you should ever use a general or binary tree. Even binary search trees that allow you to search for data logarithmically are slower than hash tables, so why should you ever use trees? Trees enable you to store hierarchical information that would be difficult or impossible to represent in a linear data structure like an array. For example, imagine you wanted to represent the directories on your computer programmatically. You may have a Documents folder with 10 folders in it, and each of those folders has 20 folders in it, and each of those folders has 4 folders in it, etc. Representing the relationship between folders on your computer and what directory a user is in would be confusing and challenging to do using an array, but with a tree, it is easy (Figure 14.8).

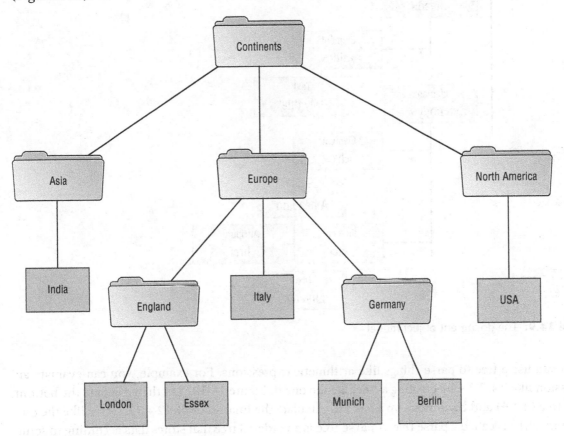

Figure 14.8: An example of folders in a tree

HTML and XML documents are another example of hierarchical data computer scientists represent with trees. **HTML** is a markup language you can use to create web pages. **XML** is a markup language for documents. You can nest HTML and XML tags, so programmers often store them as trees where each node represents a single element in the HTML or XML. When you are programming the front end of a website, the programming language JavaScript gives you access to the document object model (DOM). The **document object model** is a language-independent interface that models an XML or HTML document as a tree (Figure 14.9).

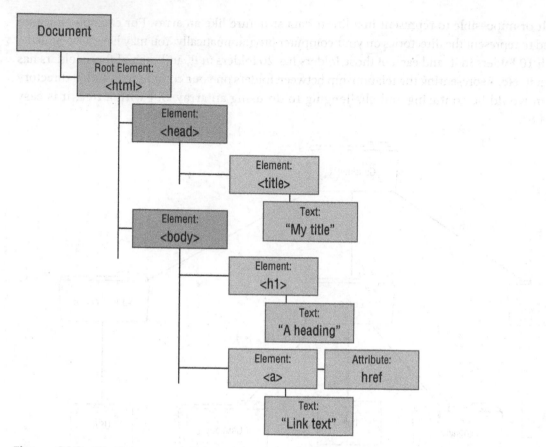

Figure 14.9: The document object model

You can use a tree to parse things like arithmetic expressions. For example, you can evaluate an expression like 2 + 3 * 4 by creating a tree like the one in Figure 14.10. You then evaluate the bottom of the tree (3 * 4) and then move up a level to calculate the final solution (2 + 7). A tree like the one in Figure 14.10 is called a parse tree. A **parse tree** is an ordered tree that stores data according to some type of syntax, like the rules for evaluating an expression.

2 + 3 * 4 =

Figure 14.10: A tree for evaluating a mathematical expression

Representing hierarchal data isn't the only reason computer scientists use trees. As you already know, you can search a sorted binary tree in logarithmic time. While a logarithmic search isn't as fast as a constant time lookup in a hash table, binary search trees offer a few advantages over hash tables. The first advantage is memory use. Because of collisions, hash tables can be 10 or more times larger than the amount of data you store in them. Binary search trees, on the other hand, do not consume any additional memory. Also, a binary search tree allows you to quickly traverse your data in both sorted and reverse sorted order, whereas you cannot traverse a hash table in sorted or reverse sorted order because hash tables don't store data in order.

Creating a Binary Tree

Here is how to create a binary tree in Python:

```python
class BinaryTree:
    def __init__(self, value):
        self.key = value
        self.left_child = None
        self.right_child = None

    def insert_left(self, value):
        if self.left_child == None:
            self.left_child = BinaryTree(value)
        else:
            bin_tree = BinaryTree(value)
            bin_tree.left_child = self.left_child
            self.left_child = bin_tree

    def insert_right(self, value):
        if self.right_child == None:
            self.right_child = BinaryTree(value)
        else:
            bin_tree = BinaryTree(value)
            bin_tree.right_child = self.right_child
            self.right_child = bin_tree
```

First, you define a class called `BinaryTree` to represent your tree. `BinaryTree` has three instance variables: `key`, `left_child`, and `right_child`. The variable `key` holds the node's data (for instance, an integer), `left_child` keeps track of the node's left child, and `right_child` keeps track of its right child. When you create a child node for your tree, you create a new instance of your `BinaryTree` class, which also has a key, a left child, and a right child. Every child node is a subtree. A **subtree** is a node in a tree, other than the root node, and its descendants. A subtree can have subtrees.

Next, you define a method called `insert_left` to create a child node and insert it into the left side of your tree.

```
def insert_left(self, value):
    if self.left_child = None:
        self.left_child = BinaryTree(value)
    else:
        bin_tree = BinaryTree(value)
        bin_tree.left_child = self.right_child
        bin_tree.left_child = bin_tree
```

First, your method checks to see whether `self.left_child` is `None`. If it is, you create a new `BinaryTree` class and assign it to `self.left_child`.

```
if self.left_child = None:
    self.left_child = BinaryTree(value)
```

Otherwise, you create a new `BinaryTree` object, assign whatever `BinaryTree` object is currently at `self.left_child` to the new `BinaryTree`'s `self.left_child`, and then assign the new `BinaryTree` to `self.left_child`.

```
else:
    bin_tree = BinaryTree(value)
    bin_tree.left_child = self.left_child
    self.left_child = bin_tree
```

After defining the `insert_left` method, you also define a method called `insert_right`, which does the same thing as `insert_left` but adds a new node to the right side of your binary tree instead.

```
def insert_right(self, value):
    if self.right_child == None:
        self.right_child = BinaryTree(value)
    else:
        bin_tree = BinaryTree(value)
        bin_tree.right_child = self.right_child
        self.right_child = bin_tree
```

Now you can create a binary tree and add nodes to it like this:

```
tree = BinaryTree(1)
tree.insert_left(2)
tree.insert_right(3)
tree.insert_left(4)
tree.left_child.insert_right(6)
tree.insert_right(5)
```

This code creates the binary tree in Figure 14.11.

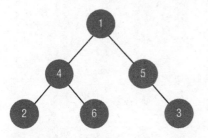

Figure 14.11: A binary tree with five nodes

Breadth-First Tree Traversal

As you learned earlier, you cannot always traverse a tree by moving from node to node without back-tracking. That doesn't mean you cannot search a tree for data, though. To search a tree for a piece of data, you need to visit every node in your tree and see if it contains the information you are looking for. There are several ways to visit each node in a binary tree. One way is a **breadth-first traversal**: a method of visiting every node in a tree by visiting each node in it level by level. For example, in the binary tree in Figure 14.12, the root is level 0, followed by levels 1, 2, and 3.

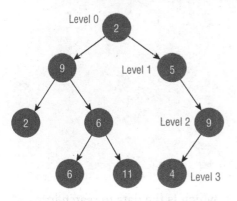

Figure 14.12: Levels in a binary tree

When you use a breadth-first traversal to perform a search, you call it a **breadth-first search**. You start a breadth-first search at the root of your tree (level 0) and go level by level through your tree, visiting each node one by one on each level until you reach the final level. You can code a breadth-first search by using two lists to track your tree's current and next level. As you visit each node in your current list, you check to see if it matches the data you are looking for and add its children to your "next" list. When it is time to move to the next level, you switch the lists. Here is how to look for a number in a binary tree using a breadth-first search:

```
class BinaryTree:
    def __init__(self, value):
        self.key = value
        self.left_child = None
        self.right_child = None

    def insert_left(self, value):
        if self.left_child == None:
            self.left_child = BinaryTree(value)
        else:
            bin_tree = BinaryTree(value)
            bin_tree.left_child = self.left_child
            self.left_child = bin_tree

    def insert_right(self, value):
        if self.right_child == None:
            self.right_child = BinaryTree(value)
        else:
            bin_tree = BinaryTree(value)
            bin_tree.right_child = self.right_child
            self.right_child = bin_tree

    def breadth_first_search(self, n):
        current = [self]
        next = []
        while current:
            for node in current:
                if node.key == n:
                    return True
                if node.left_child:
                    next.append(node.left_child)
                if node.right_child:
                    next.append(node.right_child)
            current = next
            next = []
        return False
```

Your method, `breadth_first_search`, takes one parameter, n, which is the data to search for:

```
def breadth_first_search(self, n):
```

Next, you define two lists. You use the first list, `current`, to keep track of the nodes in the current level you are searching. You use the second list, `next`, to keep track of the nodes in the next level. You also add `self` to `current`, so your algorithm starts by searching your tree's root (level zero).

```
current = [self]
next = []
```

Your `while` loop continues as long as `current` still contains nodes to search.

```
while current:
```

Then you use a `for` loop to iterate through every node in `current`.

```
for node in current:
```

If the node's value matches `n` (the value you are searching for), you return `True`.

```
if node.key == n:
    return True
```

Otherwise, you append the node's left and right child nodes to your `next` list, if they're not `None`, so they get searched when you search the next level.

```
if node.left_child:
    next.append(node.left_child)
if node.right_child:
    next.append(node.right_child)
```

Then, at the end of your `while` loop, you swap your lists `current` and `next`. The list of nodes to search next becomes the list of nodes to search now, and you set `next` to an empty list.

```
current = next
next = []
```

If your `while` loop terminates, you return `False` because your breadth-first search did not find `n` in the tree.

```
return False
```

More Tree Traversals

A breadth-first traversal is not the only way to traverse a binary tree: you can also do a depth-first traversal. In a **depth-first traversal**, you visit all the nodes in a binary tree by going as deep as you can in one direction before moving to the next sibling. Depth-first traversal offers three ways to visit every node: preorder, postorder, and in order. The implementations of the three approaches are similar, but their uses are different.

Say you have a binary tree shown in Figure 14.13. In preorder traversal, you start with the root and move to the left and then to the right.

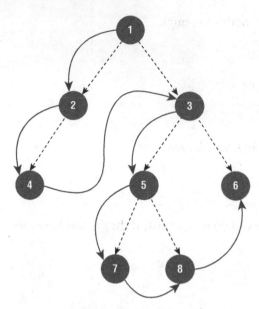

Preorder: 1, 2, 4, 3, 5, 7, 8, 6

Figure 14.13: A book represented as a tree

Here is the code for a preorder tree traversal:

```
def preorder(tree):
    if tree:
        print(tree.key)
        preorder(tree.left_child)
        preorder(tree.right_child)
```

Your function recursively calls itself until it hits its base case, which is this line of code:

```
if tree:
```

This line of code prints each tree node's value:

```
print(tree.key)
```

And these lines of code call `preorder` on each tree node's left child and right child:

```
        preorder(tree.left_child)
        preorder(tree.right_child)
```

This traversal should be familiar to you because it is similar to what you did when you wrote merge sort in Chapter 4. When you coded the merge sort, you put a recursive call to the left half of a list followed by a recursive call to the right half of a list. Your algorithm called itself with the left half until you had a list with only one item. Your algorithm called your recursive code to break up your right half of the list whenever that happened. When you hit your base case, you moved up a level in your recursive stack and merged the two lists with the code you wrote underneath your two recursive calls. Your merge sort algorithm is similar to a preorder traversal but is called a *postorder traversal*. The difference between a postorder traversal and a preorder traversal is that you print each node's value (or do something else) after your recursive calls in a postorder traversal.

```
def postorder(tree):
    if tree:
        postorder(tree.left_child)
        postorder(tree.right_child)
        print(tree.key)
```

With a postorder traversal, you move through a tree starting on the left, then moving to the right, and ending with the root, as shown in Figure 14.14.

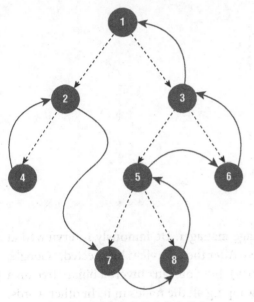

Postorder: 4, 2, 7, 8, 5, 6, 3, 1

Figure 14.14: A postorder tree traversal

If you imagine a postorder traversal as your merge sort algorithm, you print a node every time you make a merge.

Finally, you have an in-order traversal.

```
def inorder(tree):
    if tree:
        inorder (tree.left_child)
        print(tree.key)
        inorder (tree.right_child)
```

An in-order traversal is like a preorder and postorder traversal, but you print the node's value (or do something else) in between your two recursive calls. When you use an in-order traversal, you move through a tree from the left to the root to the right, as shown in Figure 14.15.

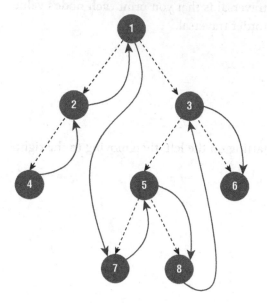

Inorder: 4, 2, 1, 7, 5, 8, 3, 6

Figure 14.15: An in-order tree traversal

Invert a Binary Tree

Max Howell is the creator of Homebrew, a popular package manager. He famously interviewed at Google for a position as a software engineer and was rejected. After the interview, he tweeted, "Google: 90% of our engineers use the software you wrote (Homebrew), but you can't invert a binary tree on a whiteboard, so ##$$ off." **Inverting a binary tree** means swapping all the nodes in it. In other words, every right node becomes a left node, and every left node becomes a right node. In this section, you will learn how to invert a binary tree, so you don't end up like Max Howell in a technical interview.

To invert a binary tree, you need to visit every node on it and keep track of each node's children so that you can swap them. One way to accomplish this is using a breadth-first search, which allows you to easily keep track of each left and right child and switch them.

Here is the code to invert a binary tree:

```
class BinaryTree:
    def __init__(self, value):
        self.key = value
        self.left_child = None
```

```
        self.right_child = None

    def insert_left(self, value):
        if self.left_child == None:
            self.left_child = BinaryTree(value)
        else:
            bin_tree = BinaryTree(value)
            bin_tree.left_child = self.left_child
            self.left_child = bin_tree

    def insert_right(self, value):
        if self.right_child == None:
            self.right_child = BinaryTree(value)
        else:
            bin_tree = BinaryTree(value)
            bin_tree.right_child = self.right_child
            self.right_child = bin_tree

    def invert(self):
        current = [self]
        next = []
        while current:
            for node in current:
                if node.left_child:
                    next.append(node.left_child)
                if node.right_child:
                    next.append(node.right_child)
                tmp = node.left_child
                node.left_child = node.right_child
                node.right_child = tmp
            current = next
            next = []
```

The code is the same as your breadth-first traversal to search for a number, but instead of checking whether a node's value is n, you swap the right and left child each iteration.

To accomplish this, you have to first save node.left_child in a temporary variable called tmp. Then, you set node.left_child to node.right_child and node.right_child to tmp, which swaps the two child nodes.

```
tmp = node.left_child
node.left_child = node.right_child
node.right_child = tmp
```

When your algorithm finishes, you have successfully inverted your binary tree.

Another, more elegant way to invert a binary tree is to use a depth-first traversal, which you can try in the challenges.

Vocabulary

tree: A nonlinear abstract data type made up of nodes connected in a hierarchical structure.

root node: The top node of a tree.

child node: A node connected to a parent node above it in a tree.

parent node: A node with one or more child nodes.

sibling nodes: Nodes that share the same parent.

edge: The connection between two nodes in a tree.

leaf node: A node without child nodes.

branch node: A node with child nodes.

binary tree: A tree data structure where each node can have only two children.

binary search tree: A tree data structure where each node can have only two children, and the tree stores its nodes in sorted order where every node's value is greater than its left child's value and lower than its right child's value.

descendants: A node's children and their children and their children's children, etc.

HTML: A markup language you can use to create web pages.

XML: A markup language for documents.

document object model: A language-independent interface that models an XML or HTML document as a tree.

parse tree: An ordered tree that stores data according to some type of syntax, like the rules for evaluating an expression.

subtree: A node in a tree, other than the root node, and its descendants.

breadth-first traversal: A method of visiting every node in a tree by visiting each node in it level by level.

breadth-first search: When you use a breadth-first traversal to perform a search.

depth-first traversal: Visiting all the nodes in a binary tree by going as deep as you can in one direction before moving to the next sibling.

inverting a binary tree: Swapping all of the nodes in it.

Challenges

1. Add a method called `has_leaf_nodes` to your binary tree code. The method should return `True` if the tree has no leaf nodes and `False` if it does not.
2. Invert a binary tree using a depth-first traversal.

15 Binary Heaps

The rise of Google, the rise of Facebook, the rise of Apple, I think are proof that there is a place for computer science as something that solves problems that people face every day.

Eric Schmidt

A **priority queue** is an abstract data type that describes a data structure where each piece of data has a priority. Unlike a queue that releases items on a first-come, first-served basis, a priority queue serves elements by priority. It removes the data with the highest priority first, followed by the subsequent highest priority data (or the opposite with the smallest value coming first). A heap is one of many priority queue implementations. A **heap** is a tree-based data structure in which each node keeps track of two pieces of information: a value and its priority. You call a heap node's value a **key**. While a node's key and its priority can be unrelated, if its data is a numerical value, such as an integer or a character, you can also use it as its priority. In this chapter, I use the key in the heaps you will see also to represent priority.

Computer scientists build heaps using trees. There are many types of heaps (depending on what kind of tree you use to create your heap), but you will learn about binary heaps in this chapter. A **binary heap** is a heap that you create using a binary tree (Figure 15.1).

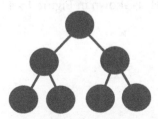

Figure 15.1: You create a binary heap using a binary tree.

There are two types of binary heaps: max heaps and min heaps. A **max heap's** parent node's priority is always greater than or equal to any child node's priority, and the node with the highest priority is the tree's root. For example, Figure 15.2 shows a max heap with the integers 1, 2, 3, 4, 6, 8, and 10.

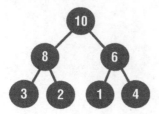

Figure 15.2: A max heap has the highest priority node as the root.

A **min heap's** parent node's priority is always less than or equal to any child node's priority, and the node with the lowest priority is the root of the tree. Figure 15.3 shows a min heap with the same integers as the max heap from Figure 15.2.

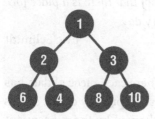

Figure 15.3: A min heap has the lowest priority node as the root.

In a binary heap, the ordering (min or max) applies only to a parent node and its children. There is no sorting between sibling nodes. As you can see in Figure 15.3, the siblings are not in order (6 and 4).

Computer scientists call creating a heap from a data structure like an array **heapifying**. For example, let's say you have an array of unsorted keys like this:

```
["R", "C", "T", "H", "E", "D", "L"]
```

To heapify this data, first, you add each piece of data as a node to a binary tree. You start at the top of your tree and then fill in child nodes left to right on each subsequent level, as shown in Figure 15.4.

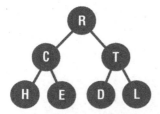

Figure 15.4: The result of heapifying an array

Then, you balance your heap. **Balancing a heap** means reordering keys that are out of order. In this case, you start with the last parent node (T) and compare it with its leaf nodes. If any of the leaf nodes have a value smaller than that of the parent node, you swap it with the parent node (Figure 15.5).

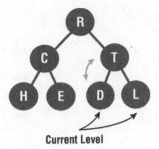

Current Level

Figure 15.5: Swapping values to balance a heap

In this case, D is the smallest of the three nodes (T, D, and L), so you swap it with its parent node T.

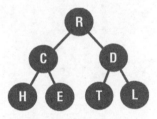

Figure 15.6: Swapping D and T is the first step to balance this heap.

Next, you move to the next-last parent and its leaf nodes (C, H, and E). C comes before both H and E, so you don't make any swaps on the left side of the tree (Figure 15.7).

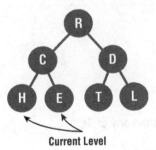

Current Level

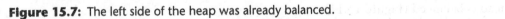

Figure 15.7: The left side of the heap was already balanced.

Now, you move up a level and compare again (Figure 15.8).

C has the lowest value of the nodes R, C, and D, so you swap C with R. Now C is the tree's root (Figure 15.9).

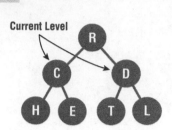

Figure 15.8: Balancing the tree at the next level

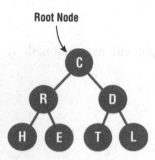

Figure 15.9: C is now the root node in your binary heap.

Now you "trickle down" the R node by comparing its value with its leaf nodes. If the R node has a value larger than one of its leaf nodes, you swap them and compare R node's value with its new leaf nodes. You continue this as long as R either has a value larger than any of its leaf nodes or you reach the lowest level of the heap. E comes before R, so you swap them (Figure 15.10).

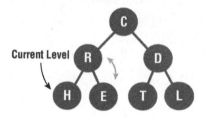

Figure 15.10: The R node trickles down the tree as long as it has a larger value than any of its leaf nodes.

Now, your heap is balanced (Figure 15.11).

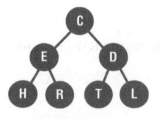

Figure 15.11: A balanced heap

Computer scientists often store heaps in arrays. You can store a heap in a Python list by distributing the keys into a list based on their position in the tree (Figure 15.12).

C	E	D	H	R	T	L

[0] [1] [2] [3] [4] [5] [6]

Figure 15.12: An array with keys at indexes based on their position in the tree.

Inside of your list, your heap's root node is at index 0. Its left child is at index 1, and its right child node is at index 2. You can use a mathematical equation to find the position of a node's child. For any node, k, its left child's index is $2k + 1$, and the right child's index is $2k + 2$. For example, the equation to find the right child of C is $2 * 0 + 2$, which equals 2. That means the right child for the node at index 0 is at index 2 (Figure 15.13).

[0]   [2]

Figure 15.13: The right child of the root is at index 2.

When to Use Heaps

You can find the maximum or minimum value in a max or min heap in constant time, but removing the minimum node from a min heap or the maximum node from a max heap is logarithmic because after you remove the item, you have to balance the remaining nodes. Inserting data into a heap is logarithmic, and searching for data in a heap is O(n).

Heaps are helpful anytime you have to execute tasks according to priority. For example, your operating system could use a heap to keep track of different tasks and allocate resources depending on each task's priority. You can also use a heap to implement Dijkstra's algorithm for finding the shortest path between two nodes in a graph. Dijkstra's algorithm, which you will learn about in Chapter 16, can help you solve routing problems, like determining how to get from one city to another and routing in computer networks. Computer scientists also use heaps in a sorting algorithm called *heapsort*.

Creating a Heap

Python has a library function called `heapq` that makes it easy to create a min heap. Here is a program that uses the `heapify` function from `heapq` to heapify a list of seven elements:

```
from heapq import heapify

a_list = ['R', 'C', 'T', 'H', 'E', 'D', 'L']
heapify(a_list)
```

```
print(a_list)

>> ['C', 'E', 'D', 'H', 'R', 'T', 'L']
```

First, you import the `heapify` function from the `heapq` library. Then you pass a list to the `heapify` function. As you can see, when you print your heapified list, it is now a min heap you are storing in a Python list.

You can use the `heapq` library's function `heappop` to extract a key from a heap and rebalance it. Here's how to remove the root key from a heap and balance its remaining keys:

```
from heapq import heapify, heappop

a_list = ['R', 'C', 'T', 'H', 'E', 'D', 'L']
heap = heapify(a_list)
print(a_list)
heappop(a_list)
print("After popping")
print(a_list)

>> ['C', 'E', 'D', 'H', 'R', 'T', 'L']
>> After popping
>> ['D', 'E', 'L', 'H', 'R', 'T']
```

First, you import both `heapify` and `heappop` from the `heapq` module:

```
from heapq import heapify, heappop
```

Then, you create a heap by passing your list to the `heapify` function and print it:

```
a_list = ['R', 'C', 'T', 'H', 'E', 'D', 'L']
heap = heapify(a_list)
print(a_list)
```

Next, you use the `heappop` function to pop the minimum element from your heap and print the result:

```
heappop(a_list)
print("After popping")
print(a_list)
```

You can use a `while` loop to pop all the elements off a heap. Here is how to create a heap and pop all of its keys off:

```
from heapq import heapify, heappop

a_list = ['D', 'E', 'L', 'H', 'R', 'T']
heapify(a_list)
while len(a_list) > 0:
    print(heappop(a_list))
```

First, you create a heap:

```
a_list = ['D', 'E', 'L', 'H', 'R', 'T']
heapify(a_list)
```

Then, you use a `while` loop to pop all of its keys:

```
while len(a_list) > 0:
    print(heappop(a_list))
```

The `heapq` library also has a function called `heappush` that inserts a key into a heap and rebalances it. Here is how to use `heappush` to push an item onto your heap:

```
from heapq import heapify, heappush


a_list = ['D', 'E', 'L', 'H', 'R', 'T']
heapify(a_list)
heappush(a_list, "Z")
print(a_list)

>> ['D', 'E', 'L', 'H', 'R', 'T', 'Z']
```

Python only provides a built-in function for min heaps, but you can easily create a max heap for numeric values by multiplying each value by –1. A max heap with strings as keys is more challenging to implement. Instead of using the `heapq` library, you have to create one using a class or code a heap yourself.

Finally, you can use `heapq` to handle priority-value pairs by storing tuples whose first element is the priority and the second element is the value, which could be anything. You will see an example of this in the next chapter when you code Dikijstras algorithm.

Connecting Ropes with Minimal Cost

You can use heaps to solve many problems that come up in your day-to-day programming as well as the ones that show up in technical interviews. For example, in a technical interview, you may be given a list of different rope lengths and asked to connect all of the ropes, two at a time, in the order that results in the lowest total cost. The cost of connecting two ropes is their sum, and the total cost is the sum of connecting all the ropes. So, for example, say you were given this list of ropes:

```
[5, 4, 2, 8]
```

First, you could connect 8 and 2, then 4 and 10, and then 5 and 14. When you add up each cost, then, you get 43.

```
[5, 4, 2, 8] # 8 + 2 = 10
[5, 4, 10] # 10 + 4 = 14
[5, 14] # 5 + 14 = 19
# 10 + 14 + 19 = 43
```

However, if you connect the ropes in a different order, you get a different answer. To get the correct answer, you need to connect the two smallest ropes each time, like this:

```
[5, 4, 2, 8] # 4 + 2 = 6
[5, 8, 6] # 6 + 5 = 11
[8, 11] # 8 + 11 = 19
# 6 + 11 + 19 = 36
```

The total cost when you approach the problem like this is 36, which is the correct answer.

You can use a min heap to write a function that solves this problem. Here is how to do it:

```
from heapq import heappush, heappop, heapify


def find_min_cost(ropes):
    heapify(ropes)
    cost = 0
    while len(ropes) > 1:
        sum = heappop(ropes) + heappop(ropes)
        heappush(ropes, sum)
        cost += sum
    return cost
```

First you define a function `find_min_cost` that takes your list of ropes as a parameter:

```
def find_min_cost(ropes):
```

Then, you use `heapify` to turn `ropes` into a min heap and define a variable called `cost` to keep track of the total cost of adding all of the ropes.

```
heapify(ropes)
cost = 0
```

Next, you create a `while` loop that runs as long as the length of `ropes` is greater than 1.

```
while len(ropes) > 1:
```

Inside of your loop you use `heappop` to get the two lowest values from your heap and add them up. Then you use `heappush` to push their sum back onto your heap. Finally, you add their sum to cost.

```
sum = heappop(ropes) + heappop(ropes)
heappush(ropes, sum)
cost += sum
```

When your loop ends, you return `cost`, which contains the lowest cost for connecting all the ropes.

```
return cost
```

Vocabulary

priority queue: An abstract data type that describes a data structure where each piece of data has a priority.

heap: A tree-based data structure where each node keeps track of two data pieces: the data itself and its priority.

key: The value of a node in a heap.

binary heap: A heap that uses a binary tree as its underlying data structure.

max heap: A heap where the parent node's priority is always greater than or equal to any child node's priority, and the node with the highest priority is the tree's root.

min heap: A heap where the parent node's priority is always less than or equal to any child node's priority, and the node with the lowest priority is the root of the tree.

heapifying: Creating a heap from a data structure like an array.

balancing a heap: Reordering keys that are out of order.

Challenge

1. Write a function that can accept a binary tree as a parameter and return `True` if it is a min heap and `False` if not.

16 Graphs

Learning to code will be a huge booster for your future, no matter what your professional plans may be. Learning to code will also make you extremely cool!

Max Levchin

A **graph** is an abstract data type in which a piece of data connects to one or more other pieces of data. Each piece of data in a graph is called a **vertex** or a *node*. A vertex has a name called a *key*. A vertex can have additional data called its **payload**. The connection between vertices in a graph is called an **edge**. A graph's edges can contain a **weight**: the cost to travel between vertices. For example, if you created a graph representing the data in a map, each vertex could be a city, and the weight between two vertices could be the distance between them (Figure 16.1).

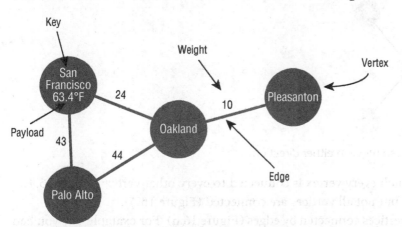

Figure 16.1: A graph contains vertices, edges, payloads, and weight.

There are several types of graphs, including directed graphs, undirected graphs, and complete graphs. A **directed graph** is one in which each edge has a direction associated with it, and you can move between two vertices only in that direction. The connection between two vertices is typically in one direction, but you can also make an edge a two-way connection. A directed graph is an excellent choice for creating a graph representing a social network with followers (like Twitter). For example, you could use a directed graph to represent that you are following Lebron James on Twitter, but he is not following you back. When you are drawing a directed graph, you typically represent the edges with arrows showing the direction you can move (Figure 16.2).

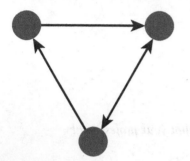

Figure 16.2: A directed graph moves in a specific direction.

An **undirected graph** is one in which the edges are bidirectional, which means you can travel in either direction between two connected vertices. You can think of this as a two-way connection, such as the relationship between friends on a social network like Facebook. For example, if Logan is friends with Hadley on Facebook, then Hadley is friends with Logan. When you are drawing an undirected graph, you usually draw the edges without arrows (Figure 16.3).

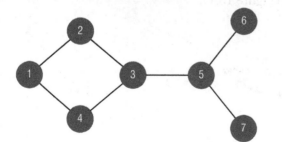

Figure 16.3: An undirected graph can move in either direction.

A **complete graph** is one in which every vertex is connected to every other vertex (Figure 16.4). In an **incomplete graph**, some but not all vertices are connected (Figure 16.5).

A graph **path** is a sequence of vertices connected by edges (Figure 16.6). For example, say you had a graph representing a city. A path between Los Angeles and San Francisco would be a series of edges (representing roads) you can use to travel from Los Angeles to San Francisco.

A **cycle** is a path in a graph starting and ending at the same vertex. An **acyclic graph** is a graph that does not contain a cycle. See Figure 16.7.

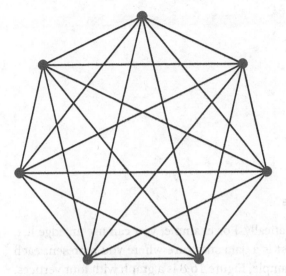

Figure 16.4: A complete graph has connections among all vertices.

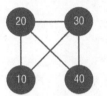

Figure 16.5: An incomplete graph has some connected vertices.

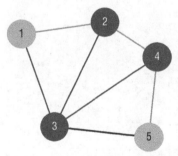

Figure 16.6: A graph path follows a specific sequence.

Many of these concepts should already be familiar to you because you've already learned about trees. A tree is a restricted form of a graph. Trees have direction (the parent-child relationship) and do not contain cycles, which makes them directed acyclic graphs with a restriction: a child can have only one parent.

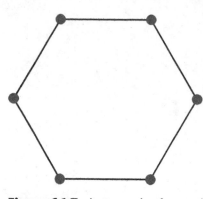

Figure 16.7: An example of a graph that contains a cycle

There are several ways to create graphs programmatically. For example, you can use an edge list, an adjacency matrix, or an adjacency list. An **edge list** is a data structure where you represent each edge in a graph with two vertices that connect. For example, Figure 16.8 is a graph with four vertices.

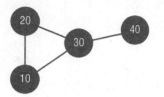

Figure 16.8: A graph with four vertices

You can represent it with an edge list like this:

```
[
[10, 20]
[10, 30]
[20, 10]
[20, 30]
[30, 10]
[30, 20]
[30, 40]
[40, 30]
]
```

This edge list is a list of lists, and each list contains two vertices from the graph that connect.

You can also represent a graph with an adjacency matrix. An **adjacency matrix** is a two-dimensional array of rows and columns that contains a graph's vertices. In an adjacency matrix, you use the intersection of each row and column to represent an edge. Traditionally, you use a 1 to represent vertices that connect and a 0 to show vertices that do not. When two vertices are connected, they are **adjacent**. Figure 16.9 shows how you represent the same graph with an adjacency matrix:

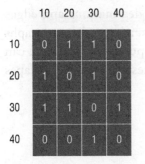

Figure 16.9: An adjacency matrix of the graph in Figure 16.8

One problem with adjacency matrices is sparsity or empty cells. There are eight empty cells in this example. Adjacency matrices are not a very efficient way to store data because they can end up with a large number of empty cells, which is an inefficient use of your computer's memory.

Finally, you can also represent a graph with an adjacency list. An **adjacency list** is a collection of unordered lists, with each list representing the connections for a single vertex. Here is the same graph from Figure 16.8 as an adjacency list:

```
{
10: [20, 30],
20: [10, 30],
30: [10, 20, 40],
40: [30]
}
```

As you can see, the node 10 connects to 20 and 30, the node 20 connects to 10 and 30, and so on.

When to Use Graphs

As you already know, there are many different graph implementations. Adding a vertex and an edge to a graph is generally O(1). The run time for searching, deleting, and other algorithms in a graph depends on the graph's implementation and which data structures you used to implement the graph: arrays, linked lists, hash tables, etc. In general, the performance of basic operations on graphs depends on either the number of vertices in the graph, the number of edges in the graph, or some combination of those two numbers since graphs essentially deal with two things: items in the graph (vertices) and connections (edges) between those items.

Graphs are helpful in many situations. For example, software engineers at social media companies like Instagram and Twitter use vertices in a graph to represent people and edges to represent the associations between them. Programmers also use graphs to build networks, often representing the devices on it as vertices with the edges representing wireless or wired links between those devices. You can use graphs to create maps with each vertex representing cities and other destinations and edges representing roads, bus routes, or air routes between those destinations. Programmers also use graphs to find the fastest path between destinations. They are also helpful for computer graphics. You can use the vertices and edges of graphs to represent the points, lines, and planes of 2D and 3D shapes (Figure 16.10).

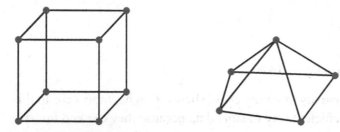

Figure 16.10: Graphs can represent 3D shapes.

Search engine algorithms often use graphs to help determine search ranking based on the connectivity of the search and results. Operating systems and programming language systems also use graphs in memory management.

Creating a Graph

Here is how to create an adjacency list in Python:

```
class Vertex:
    def __init__(self, key):
        self.key = key
        self.connections = {}

    def add_adj(self, vertex, weight=0):
        self.connections[vertex] = weight

    def get_connections(self):
        return self.connections.keys()

    def get_weight(self, vertex):
        return self.connections[vertex]


class Graph:
    def __init__(self):
        self.vertex_dict = {}

    def add_vertex(self, key):
        new_vertex = Vertex(key)
```

```
        self.vertex_dict[key] = new_vertex

    def get_vertex(self, key):
        if key in self.vertex_dict:
            return self.vertex_dict[key]
        return None

    def add_edge(self, f, t, weight=0):
        if f not in self.vertex_dict:
            self.add_vertex(f)
        if t not in self.vertex_dict:
            self.add_vertex(t)
        self.vertex_dict[f].add_adj(self.vertex_dict[t], weight)
```

First, you define a vertex class, as you did earlier with nodes when you created linked lists:

```
class Vertex:
    def __init__(self, key):
        self.key = key
        self.connections = {}

    def add_adj(self, vertex, weight=0):
        self.connections[vertex] = weight
```

Your Vertex class has two instance variables: self.key and self.connections. The first variable, key, represents the vertex's key, and the second variable, connections, is a dictionary where you will store the vertices each vertex is adjacent to.

```
def __init__(self, key):
    self.key = key
    self.connections = {}
```

Your Vertex class has a method called add_adj that accepts a vertex as a parameter and makes it adjacent to the vertex you called the method on by adding the connection to self.connections. The method also accepts a weight as a parameter if you want to add a weight to the relationship.

```
def add_adj(self, vertex, weight=0):
    self.connections[vertex] = weight
```

Next, you define a class called Graph. Graph has an instance variable self.vertex_dict that stores the vertices in each graph.

```
def __init__(self):
    self.vertex_dict = {}
```

Your class's method add_vertex adds a new vertex to a graph by first creating a vertex and then mapping the key the user passes in as a parameter to the new vertex inside self.vertex_dict.

```
def add_vertex(self, key):
    new_vertex = Vertex(key)
    self.vertex_dict[key] = new_vertex
```

Your next method, `get_vertex`, accepts a key as a parameter and checks `self.vertex_dict` to see if the vertex is your graph.

```
def get_vertex(self, key):
    if key in self.vertex_dict:
        return self.vertex_dict[key]
    return None
```

Finally, your graph class has a method called `add_edge` that adds an edge between two vertices in your graph.

```
def add_edge(self, f, t, weight=0):
    if f not in self.vertex_dict:
        self.add_vertex(f)
    if t not in self.vertex_dict:
        self.add_vertex(t)
    self.vertex_dict[f].add_adj(self.vertex_dict[t], weight)
```

Now you can create a graph and add vertices to it like this:

```
graph = Graph()
graph.add_vertex("A")
graph.add_vertex("B")
graph.add_vertex("C")
graph.add_edge("A", "B", 1)
graph.add_edge("B", "C", 10)
vertex_a = graph.get_vertex("A")
vertex_b = graph.get_vertex("B")
```

In this example, to keep things simple, two different vertices cannot have the same key.

Dijkstra's Algorithm

When you are working with graphs, you often need to find the shortest path between two vertices. One of the most famous algorithms in computer science is called **Dijkstra's algorithm**, and you can use it to find the shortest path from a vertex in a graph to every other vertex. The famous computer scientist Edsger Dijkstra invented it in only 20 minutes in his head without a pen or paper.

Here is how Dijkstra's algorithm works. First, you pick a starting vertex. Your starting vertex is the vertex you will find the shortest path to every other vertex in your graph from. Say you have a graph that looks like Figure 16.11.

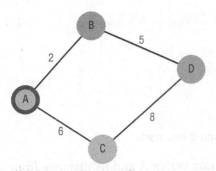

Figure 16.11: A graph with four vertices

If A is your starting vertex, at the end of your program, you will have a dictionary that contains every vertex in the graph and the shortest path from the starting vertex (A) to each vertex.

```
{
"A": 0,
"B": 2,
"C": 6,
"D": 7,
}
```

As you can see from Figure 16.11, the shortest path from A to D is 7 because vertex A to vertex B to vertex D is 7 (2 + 5), and vertex A to vertex C to vertex D is 14 (6 + 8).

At the beginning of the algorithm, you set the path from the starting vertex to itself to zero and set all the other path lengths to infinity (Figure 16.12).

Distance:

A: 0
B: ∞
C: ∞
D: ∞

Figure 16.12: Set the path to the starting vertex to zero and the other paths to infinity.

The key to your algorithm is a priority queue. You use a priority queue to do a breadth-first search through your graph. You use your priority queue to track vertices and their distances from the starting vertex. Let's take a look at how this works with the graph from earlier.

Your algorithm begins with the starting vertex A in your priority queue. You keep track of all of the shortest paths in a dictionary. In your dictionary, you set the distance from vertex A to itself to 0 and set all other distances to infinity (Figure 16.13). At this point, you haven't visited any vertices yet. Visiting a vertex means popping it off your priority queue, and if you haven't found a shorter path from the starting vertex to it, look at all the vertices adjacent to it for shorter paths to the starting vertex. If you find a shorter path, you put that adjacent vertex on your priority queue.

```
Unvisited Vertices {A, B, C, D}
Priority Queue [(0, A)]
Distances {

A: 0,
B: ∞,
C: ∞,
D: ∞,
}
```

Figure 16.13: What the data structures in your algorithm look like when it first starts

At this point your priority queue has only one vertex, so you pop vertex A and its distance from the starting vertex (0) off of your priority queue and check to see if you've already found a shorter path to this vertex. When you are looking at a new vertex from your priority queue, if you've already found a shorter path from the starting vertex to that vertex, you do not need to do anything. In this case, you haven't found a shorter path to vertex A, so you iterate through all the vertices adjacent to vertex A.

Next, you calculate the adjacent vertices' distances from the starting vertex. You do this by adding the distance you got from the priority queue to the adjacent vertex's weight (its distance from the vertex you popped off your priority queue). Because your priority queue holds two pieces of information for each vertex on it—the vertex and its distance from the starting vertex—no matter how far you get away from the starting vertex, you can easily calculate the distance between a new adjacent vertex and the starting vertex by adding the distance you got from your priority queue to the adjacent vertices' weight.

If the adjacent vertex's distance from the starting vertex is shorter than any of the paths you've found so far, you add the new path to your dictionary and put the adjacent vertex on your priority queue. In this case, you put both of the vertices adjacent to vertex A (B and C) on your priority queue and add their paths to your dictionary (Figure 16.14).

```
Unvisited Vertices {A̶, B, C, D}
Priority Queue [(2, B), (6, C)]
Distances {

A: 0,
B: 2,
C: 6,
D: ∞,
}
```

Figure 16.14: The data structures after visiting vertex A

Now, you pop the vertex B off of your priority queue because it has the highest priority (the shortest path to the starting vertex). You have not found a shorter path from B to the starting vertex yet, so you continue visiting this vertex. You check all of its adjacent vertices for shorter paths, add any shorter paths you find to your dictionary, and update your priority queue. In this case, B has only one adjacent vertex with a shorter path (D), so you update D in your dictionary to 7 and add D and its distance to the starting vertex to your priority queue (Figure 16.15).

Unvisited Vertices {A̶, B̶, C, D}
Priority Queue [(6, C) (7, D)]
Distances {

A: 0,
B: 2,
C: 6,
D: 7,
}

Figure 16.15: The data structures after visiting vertex B

Now you pop the vertex C off your priority queue because it has the shortest path in your priority queue. C is also adjacent to D, but as you saw earlier, its distance from the starting vertex is 14 and you've already found a shorter path to D, so you do not add D to your priority queue again (Figure 16.16). Ignoring longer paths (not visiting them again) is what makes this algorithm so efficient.

Unvisited Vertices {A̶, B̶, C̶, D}
Priority Queue [(7, D)]
Distances {

A: 0,
B: 2,
C: 6,
D: 7,
}

Figure 16.16: The data structures after visiting vertex C

Vertex D is not adjacent to any other vertices, so once you pop off vertex D, your algorithm is complete (Figure 16.17).

Unvisited Vertices {A̶, B̶, C̶, D̶}
Priority Queue [ ]
Distances {

A: 0,
B: 2,
C: 6,
D: 7,
}

Figure 16.17: The data structures after visiting vertex D

The following is the code to implement Dijkstra's algorithm in Python. In this case, your algorithm expects a graph as a dictionary of dictionaries rather than the Graph class you coded earlier in the chapter.

```
import heapq


def dijkstra(graph, starting_vertex):
    distances = {vertex: float('infinity') for vertex in graph}
    distances[starting_vertex] = 0
```

```
        pq = [(0, starting_vertex)]

        while len(pq) > 0:
            current_distance, current_vertex = heapq.heappop(pq)
            if current_distance > distances[current_vertex]:
                continue

            for neighbor, weight in graph[current_vertex].items():
                distance = current_distance + weight
                if distance < distances[neighbor]:
                    distances[neighbor] = distance
                    heapq.heappush(pq, (distance, neighbor))
        return distances


graph = {
    'A': {'B': 2, 'C': 6},
    'B': {'D': 5},
    'C': {'D': 8},
    'D': {},
}

dijkstra(graph, 'A')
print(dijkstra(graph, 'A'))
```

First, you import `heapq` because your algorithm uses a heap as a priority queue. Your function `dijkstra` returns a dictionary containing the shortest paths from the starting vertex. Your function takes two parameters: a graph and the vertex you want to find the shortest paths from.

```
import heapq


def dijkstra(graph, starting_vertex):
```

In this implementation, you will pass in an adjacency list like this:

```
graph = {
    'A': {'B': 2, 'C': 6},
    'B': {'D': 5},
    'C': {'D': 8},
    'D': {},
}
```

When you call your function `dijkstra`, you pass in the graph and a string to represent a starting vertex like this:

```
dijkstra(graph, 'A')
```

The starting vertex must be a vertex in the graph.

Inside your function, you create a dictionary called `distances` to hold the paths from the starting vertex to each other vertex in the graph. At the end of the algorithm, this dictionary will contain the shortest path from the starting vertex to every other vertex. You create the dictionary using a dictionary comprehension: similar to a list comprehension but for dictionaries. Your dictionary comprehension maps each vertex to `float('infinity')`: Python's representation of infinity. You map each vertex to infinity because your algorithm compares the lengths of paths and the paths start as unknown, so you use infinity to represent that.

```
distances = {vertex: float('infinity') for vertex in graph}
```

When you pass in the dictionary (representing a graph) from earlier to `dijkstra`, the previous code produces a dictionary that looks like this:

```
{'A': inf, 'B': inf, 'C': inf, 'D': inf}
```

Next, you set the distance from the starting vertex (the vertex you are finding all of the shortest paths from) to itself to zero since the distance between a vertex and itself is zero.

```
distances[starting_vertex] = 0
```

Next, you create a list (you will use as a priority queue) that initially holds the starting vertex and its distance from the starting vertex (zero):

```
pq = [(0, starting_vertex)]
```

Next comes your code to visit the vertices on your priority queue. You use a `while` loop that runs as long as there is still one or more vertices left in the priority queue. You use this `while` loop to visit all the vertices in your graph.

```
while len(pq) > 0:
```

Inside your `while` loop, you pop the distance from the starting vertex and the current vertex from your priority queue and save them in the variables `current_distance` and `current_vertex`. The current vertex is the vertex in the priority queue that has the shortest distance from the starting vertex. Your priority queue automatically serves you the vertex with the shortest distance whenever you pop a new vertex off it (because your priority queue is a min heap).

```
current_distance, current_vertex = heapq.heappop(pq)
```

You want to process a vertex only if you haven't already found a shorter path from that vertex to the starting vertex. That is why next, you check to see if the current distance from the starting vertex is greater than a distance you've already recorded in your `distances` dictionary. If it is greater, you don't care about that path because you've already logged a shorter path, so you use the `continue` keyword to jump back to the top of your `while` loop and examine another vertex (if there is one) instead.

```
if current_distance > distances[current_vertex]:
    continue
```

If the `current_distance` is not greater than (in other words, it is shorter than or equal to) `distances[current_vertex]`, you iterate through all of the vertices adjacent to the current vertex.

```
for neighbor, weight in graph[current_vertex].items():
```

For each adjacent vertex, you calculate its distance from the starting vertex by adding `current_distance` to its weight. This calculation works because `current_distance` represents how far from the starting vertex the current vertex is. The variable `weight` represents how far the adjacent vertex is from the current vertex, so when you add them together, you get the distance from the starting vertex.

```
distance = current_distance + weight
```

Next, you check to see if the new path you found for that adjacent vertex is shorter than the path you already have for that vertex in your `distances` dictionary. If it is, you update your dictionary with the new path. Then, you push the new distance and the vertex onto your priority queue so your algorithm can visit it.

```
if distance < distances[neighbor]:
    distances[neighbor] = distance
    heapq.heappush(pq, (distance, neighbor))
```

When you break out of your `while` loop, it means you've explored all of the vertices, and `distances` now contains the shortest path from the starting vertex to every other vertex in your graph. All that is left to do now is return `distances`.

```
return distances
```

Vocabulary

graph: An abstract data type where a piece of data connects to one or more other pieces of data.

vertex: A piece of data in a graph.

payload: Additional data in a graph vertex.

edge: The connection between vertices in a graph.

weight: The cost to travel between vertices.

directed graph: A graph where each edge has a direction associated with it, and you can move between two vertices only in that direction.

undirected graph: A type of graph where the edges are bidirectional, which means you can travel back and forth in either direction between two connected vertices.

complete graph: A graph where every vertex connects to every other vertex.

incomplete graph: A graph where some but not all vertices are not connected.

path: A sequence of vertices connected by edges.

cycle: A path in a graph starting and ending at the same vertex.

acyclic graph: A graph that does not contain a cycle.

edge list: A data structure where you represent each edge in a graph with two vertices that connect.

adjacency matrix: A two-dimensional array of rows and columns that contains a graph's vertices.

adjacent: Two or more connected vertices in a graph.

adjacency list: A collection of unordered lists, with each list representing the connections for a single vertex.

Dijkstra's algorithm: An algorithm you can use to find the shortest path from a vertex in a graph to every other vertex.

Challenge

1. Modify Dijkstra's algorithm so it only returns the path from a starting vertex to another vertex you pass in.

17 Self-Taught Inspiration: Elon Musk

Today, Elon Musk is best known for founding Tesla, Space X, and PayPal, which revolutionized their industries. But long before he became an entrepreneur and one of the richest men on the planet, Musk was driven by a simpler idea: he wanted to design video games. How did self-taught programmer Musk go from a kid playing games to a billionaire? In this chapter, you will learn about Musk's education and how his interest in gaming led him to learn to program.

Musk's education began across the world from the Los Angeles home where he resides today. Born and raised in South Africa, Musk became interested in computers when he was ten years old. Musk was a driven child who would sometimes spend 10 hours a day reading books. He was also obsessed with video games. Musk explained that his love of video games drove him to learn to program. "I thought I could make my own games. I wanted to see how games work," Musk explained. "That's what led me to learn how to program computers."

Musk started with a book on the BASIC programming language, a popular language in the 1960s, which many computers still used in the 1980s. The book offered a six-month program to learn to code, but Musk raced through the entire program in three days. It wasn't long before Musk programmed his first video game. In 1984, when he was just 12 years old, Musk created *Blastar*. The space-based shooter drew inspiration from *Alien Invaders*. In Musk's game, players shot down spaceships carrying hydrogen bombs while dodging deadly "status beams."

Musk pitched his game to *PC and Office Technology*, which offered to buy *Blastar* for $500. Musk already learned how to turn a profit in his first programming venture: an important turning point in Musk's education. *Blastar* taught Musk several vital lessons. First, he realized that after reading a book and playing around with coding, he could create his own video game. Translating his learning into a final product also brought results: at only 12 years old, Musk was making money from his programming skills.

But Musk's education did not end there. The drive that pushed Musk to learn programming continued into his teen years. At 17 years old, Musk moved from South Africa to Canada, where he planned to live with his great-uncle in Montreal. There was just one problem: the uncle had already moved to Minnesota, which Musk realized only once he reached Canada. Musk didn't give up. He had other relatives in Canada, so he bought a bus ticket and started tracking them down. It took a nearly 2,000-mile bus ride for Musk to find a second cousin who offered him a place to stay. Still a teenager, Musk worked on a farm in Saskatchewan, cut logs in Vancouver, and cleaned out boilers.

Musk described cleaning boilers in *Elon Musk: Tesla, SpaceX, and the Quest for a Fantastic Future* Ecco, Illustrated edition (January 24, 2017): "You have to put on this hazmat suit and then shimmy through this little tunnel that you can barely fit in," he explained. "Then, you have a shovel, and you take the sand and goop and other residue, which is still steaming hot, and you have to shovel it through the same hole you came through. There is no escape. Someone else on the other side has to shovel it into a wheelbarrow. If you stay in there for more than 30 minutes, you get too hot and die."

In 1989, Musk enrolled at Queen's University in Ontario. In college, Musk told a friend, "If there was a way that I could not eat, so I could work more, I would not eat. I wish there was a way to get nutrients without sitting down for a meal." Musk's drive continued to push him. He built and sold computers from his dorm room. "I could build something to suit their needs like a tricked-out gaming machine or a simple word processor that cost less than what they could get in a store," Musk related.

He also spent hours playing games like *Civilization* and thought about a career in gaming. After transferring to the University of Pennsylvania, Musk began to gravitate toward business and technology. Although gaming had been his passion since he was a boy, Musk wanted to have a larger impact on the world. "I really like computer games, but then if I made really great computer games, how much effect would that have on the world," Musk wondered. "It wouldn't have a big effect. Even though I have an intrinsic love of video games, I couldn't bring myself to do that as a career."

In college, Musk knew he was a quick learner. He was already interested in solar power, space, the internet, and electric cars. After earning bachelor's degrees in economics and physics, Musk moved to California to earn his PhD in energy physics at Stanford. Silicon Valley quickly drew Musk's attention, and he dropped out of his doctoral program after only two days.

Instead, Musk launched Zip2 Corporation, which made online city guides. He sold the company in 1999 for more than $300 million. Since then, Musk has been involved with many other successful companies, including PayPal, SpaceX, Tesla Motors, and The Boring Company. The drive that pushed Musk to learn to program on his own helped Musk become one of the most successful entrepreneurs of all time.

18 Next Steps

For most people on Earth, the digital revolution hasn't even started yet. Within the next 10 years, all that will change. Let's get the whole world coding!

Eric Schmidt

Nice work! You made it through all the technical parts of this book. Your hard work is paying off, and you are well on your path to becoming a software engineer. I want to thank you for choosing to read my book and being part of the self-taught community. I can't believe how big our community has become. It has been terrific getting the chance to meet so many inspiring people, and I cannot wait to read your success story next. In this final chapter, I will cover what you should do moving forward and provide some resources that might help you.

What's Next?

First, let's take a second to celebrate how far you've come as a self-taught programmer. You not only know how to program, you also understand many fundamental computer science concepts. You know how to write algorithms to solve various problems, and you can look at two algorithms and quickly decide which one you want to use. You can write recursive algorithms to elegantly solve problems and search and sort data in various ways. You are familiar with a variety of data structures, and you don't just know what they are: you know when to use them as well. Overall, you've become a much more knowledgeable programmer with so many new tools in your toolkit.

Not only have you significantly increased your programming knowledge, with a little bit of practice, you can pass a technical interview, which means you are well on your way to landing a job as a software engineer. So, what should you do next? That depends on how much professional programming experience you have. If you already have experience, you can skip the next section. If you don't have any experience and want to improve your odds of getting hired, read on.

Climbing the Freelance Ladder

One thing new self-taught programmers struggle with is applying for jobs without any experience. They face the classic problem: they need experience to get a job and need a job to gain experience. I've come up with a solution to this problem that my students have had a lot of success with: I call it climbing the freelance ladder. I used the same method to get a job as a software engineer at eBay without any experience at a traditional company.

Before I got my job at eBay, I worked as a freelance programmer. The key to my success was I didn't start trying to get big jobs. I started with small jobs on a platform called Elance (now Upwork). If you aren't familiar with Upwork, it is a site for freelancers. Employers looking for contract work post a project, and contractors bid to do the job. There are other sites similar to Upwork, such as `Freelancer.com` and Fiverr. My first job paid something like $25 and took me several hours: not a great hourly wage. Fortunately, the job paid me much more in experience. The client was happy with my work on the project and left me a five-star review. That made getting my next project a little bit easier. Again, I worked hard and earned another five-star review. I worked my way up to bigger and bigger projects, eventually landing thousand-dollar projects.

When I interviewed at eBay, I didn't have any prior programming experience at a traditional company; however, during my interview, I focused on talking about all the freelance projects I had worked on. My interviewers at eBay felt my freelance experience made me a great candidate, and they ended up offering me the job. If I had tried to interview there with no prior programming experience at a traditional company and without my freelance background, I doubt I would have gotten the job that kicked off my entire career.

If you want to work as a software engineer but don't have any professional experience, don't start interviewing yet. Sign up for a platform like Upwork and start trying to get any job you can, even if it pays only $25. Then, work your way up the freelance ladder by earning five-star reviews and bidding on projects that pay more and more. When you've accumulated an impressive amount of experience, you are ready to apply for your dream software engineering job at your favorite company.

How to Get an Interview

I got my first job as a software engineer through LinkedIn. LinkedIn is still a fantastic resource for getting hired. Once you've gained some experience by climbing the freelance ladder, I recommend spending time updating your LinkedIn profile. Make sure to include your freelance experience as your most recent job and put your job title as software engineer. Consider reaching out to some of the companies you did work for and asking if they would consider endorsing your programming skills on LinkedIn.

Once your LinkedIn profile is up-to-date (and your résumé is, too), it is time to start networking. I recommend picking five to ten companies where you are interested in working and reaching out to recruiters or other team members at those companies. Companies often have a shortage of engineers and offer referral bonuses to employees who refer engineers, so if you are qualified for the position, they will most likely be happy to hear from you.

You can also use a resource like Meetup.com to find groups who get together to network and meet new people, or you can directly apply for jobs using websites like Angel.co or Indeed.com.

How to Prepare for a Technical Interview

When it comes time to apply for jobs, eventually you will need to pass a technical interview. You should give yourself plenty of time to prepare for it. There is no steadfast rule, but I recommend that you give yourself at least two to three months to prepare. It also depends on how competitive the companies you are applying to are. If you are applying to one of the FAANG companies (Facebook, Amazon, Apple, Netflix, or Google/Alphabet), it is not unheard of for hopeful engineers to spend six months or more preparing for their technical assessments. If you are applying to a startup, on the other hand, you may be able to get away with preparing for only a few weeks.

I recommend dedicating at least a few hours a day to solving problems on LeetCode, one of my favorite resources for preparing for technical interviews. It has hundreds of data structure and algorithm practice problems as well as solutions.

One of the hardest parts about technical interviews is the unnatural environment they take place in. Usually, when you are programming, you don't have someone standing over your shoulder evaluating you. Programmers also are not used to solving problems in short time periods. Nevertheless, these artificial constraints are what you will face in a technical interview. Competitive programming is the best solution I've found to prepare for coding in this type of environment. Competitive programming is coding as a sport. You compete against other programmers to solve computer science problems. It is the best way to prepare for a technical interview because it prepares you for the unique conditions you will be facing: solving problems under time pressure. When I did competitive programming to prepare for a set of technical interviews, I performed significantly better than in previous times when I only prepared by practicing problems on my own. You can try a website like Codeforces when you are ready to try competitive programming.

Once you've used competitive programming to get used to solving challenging technical problems quickly, you should try a few mock interviews with a software engineer, ideally someone who has conducted an interview before. If you can't find a friend to help, you can try hiring a software engineer on a freelance platform like Upwork or on Codementor. You can hire an experienced software engineer on these platforms for around $30 to $60, and spending even a few hours practicing a mock interview is an excellent investment.

Additional Resources

As you know, computer science is an enormous topic. My goal was to write a book you would finish and cover the subjects most likely to help you in your programming careers. That means, unfortunately, I had to leave a lot of topics out of this book. In this section, I will briefly cover some of the things I left out of this book and give you resources to learn about them.

Although you learned about binary trees in this book, I did not cover other trees deeply. You may want to spend more time studying different types of trees such as binary search trees, AVL trees, and parse trees. I also did not cover every common sorting algorithm. If you are preparing for a technical interview or want to learn even more about sorting algorithms, you should consider studying heapsort, selection sort, quicksort, counting sort, and radix sort.

You can learn about all these topics and more in *Introduction to Algorithms* by Thomas H. Cormen (MIT Press, 2010). Be warned, however, that this is not an easy book to read. Now that you understand computer science basics, you will ideally find the content much easier to understand. *Computer Science Illuminated* by Nell Dale and John Lewis (Jones & Bartlett Learning, 2012) is an excellent choice for learning more about computer science subjects outside of data structures and algorithms.

Final Thoughts

Thanks for choosing to read my book. I hope you enjoyed reading it as much as I enjoyed writing it. If you have questions or comments, feel free to reach out to me in the Self-Taught Programmers Facebook group located at `https://facebook.com/groups/selftaughtprogrammers`. You can also subscribe to my newsletter to stay up-to-date with the Self-Taught community at `https://selftaught.blog`. Finally, you can keep in touch with me on social media. My handle is `@coryalthoff` on Instagram, Twitter, and Facebook. If you have a second to leave a review on Amazon, I will be eternally grateful. Each review helps sales enormously, which allows me to continue creating new educational material for self-taught programmers.

Take care!

Index